GREAT JOBS

FOR

Business Majors

Stephen Lambert

VGM Career Books

Chicago   New York   San Francisco   Lisbon   London   Madrid   Mexico City
Milan   New Delhi   San Juan   Seoul   Singapore   Sydney   Toronto

The *McGraw·Hill* Companies

Library of Congress Cataloging-in-Publication Data

Lambert, Stephen E.
   Great jobs for business majors / Stephen Lambert. — 2nd ed.
      p.   cm. — (Great jobs for)
   Includes bibliographical references and index.
   ISBN 0-07-140581-X
   1. Job hunting.   2. Business students—Employment.   I. Title.   II. Series.

   HF5382.7 .L347   2003
   650.14—dc21   2002033300

2 3 4 5 6 7 8 9 0   DOC/DOC   2 1 0 9 8 7 6 5 4

ISBN 0-07-140581-X

McGraw-Hill books are available at special quantity discounts to use as premiums and sales promotions, or for use in corporate training programs. For more information, please write to the Director of Special Sales, Professional Publishing, McGraw-Hill, Two Penn Plaza, New York, NY 10121-2298. Or contact your local bookstore.

This book is printed on acid-free paper.

". . . Knock, knock."
"Who's there?"
"Candygram!"
For Julie

Contents

Acknowledgments

Anyone following the yearly additions to the library of Great Jobs volumes is aware that with each volume in the series, the list of people deserving of appreciation increases. In writing *Great Jobs for Business Majors*, I have been continually impressed by the generosity of those I have written to, spoken with, and met. The list for this volume is far too extensive to mention each one personally, but I owe special debts of gratitude to two very special individuals.

To Kirsten Giebutowski, many thanks for her superlative editing contribution. Friends for a long time, it's been exciting to have this collaboration. Kirsten, thank you.

To my wife, Barbara Whitney Lambert, I owe a very special thanks for her reading, editing, perceptive comments, and ideas. An educator in her own right, her contributions have become an important part of this book.

Introduction

Business: All Guarantees Are Off!

One of the interesting things that happens during college is the self-labeling that occurs because of chosen majors. The art students are seen as "artistic," the computer majors as "techies," the liberal arts students as "humanists," and you, the business major, as "realistic" or "materialistic." Of course, these labels are simplifications, generalizations, and, often, just plain wrong. A major cannot and should not define who you are, or what you do for your career.

Maybe we should begin by defining some terms. Let's start with *business*. If you're a business major or are contemplating majoring in this field, you've heard others say, "Oh, I could never do a desk job," or "I have no head for figures," or "That stuff is too technical for me" and other expressions of distaste or dislike based on their perceptions of business.

They should meet the business major working at the Metropolitan Opera, the director of community relations for Disney World, the individual who buys art to furnish corporate offices, or any of the thousands of business-people whose jobs and routines are anything but routine but that are, nonetheless, the stuff of business. Hospitals, universities, art galleries, and conservation societies are among the variety of entities that are businesses.

Business is simply another term for an organized human activity that needs to be managed in order to accomplish its goals. Those activities may be technical, like a software company, or highly artistic, such as a ballet company or symphony orchestra. In fact, you would find it a challenge to identify any vital human activity that seeks to grow, that employs people, and that is engaged in any active enterprise—from education to farming to neuroscience—that does not have a business aspect.

If you haven't thought of business this way, it's an exciting new view. It means that you can look at yourself, your interests, your personality, and your particular talents and try to find some area of business activity (and the choices are almost infinite!) to fit who you are and what you are interested in. That's an exciting prospect—exciting and necessary.

It's a rough world out there. And that's a message you've encountered from many sources, from your case studies in business school to the evening news on the major networks. Employment is no longer an absolute given, and even the most talented and skilled of workers can lose their jobs through mergers, buyouts, and consolidations as businesses try to enhance profits through economies of size. To be a contender in this volatile world, you need to have a flexible definition not only of business but of yourself as a business major.

What is a business major, exactly? Compared to your liberal arts colleagues, you've had some fairly specific information delivered to you over your four years of college. You've had, for example, accounting, computer, marketing, and organizational behavior courses. You've had opportunities, through case studies, field projects, and presentations, to practice some of these skills. But you know you're not an accountant, a computer scientist, a marketer, or an organization behaviorist. What are you, then?

Think of a business major as a college graduate who has had broad exposure to all the elements that go into making up the various aspects of human economic endeavor. You've looked at all these various areas in a general way and have an equally general understanding of how these areas interact, yet you are not a specialist and probably don't feel particularly skilled in any business activity.

The jobs outlined in the five career paths covered in *Great Jobs for Business Majors* will provide an overview of some promising areas of employment. As you read these chapters, think about which of these career areas appeals to you. The appeal base will be different for each person. For you, perhaps the most important factors are the skills demanded. Or the most important factors may be the kinds of good or services you'd be working with or the activities you'd be performing. These are all good reasons for pursuing a particular career pathway.

Business majors like yourself often find comfort during their college years in thinking that their major is the most realistic—the most real world of all the possible college majors. Business majors will often boast "I'm learning something useful. I can go right to work."

The reality is that most organizations now are working so hard to stay competitive that new college graduates—even business majors—can represent a time drain these employers cannot afford in the current economic marketplace. Training takes time and money—valuable commodities in today's world. These organizations would prefer to hire individuals who will be fast off the mark and making a contribution immediately.

Of all the many majors available to a college student, business has long held the promise of being the most practical course of study, the major that offers the most real-world applications in the classroom, with course offerings that prepare students for the fastest and easiest transition to jobs after graduation.

Fortunately, much of that thinking remains sound; however, profound and far-reaching changes have been going on in the business world. The United States, once a leader in electronics manufacture, has seen much of that authority shift to the Pacific Rim. The global economy is also a shrinking economy, and everyone is seeking markets wherever they can be found.

Add to these changes important shifts in the demographics of the global workplace, bringing diversity of ethnicity, gender, and the racial spectrum to all aspects of business. This puts new emphasis and awareness on communication skills, sensitivity, discretion, cultural appreciation, styles of leadership, and team membership skills.

Though some of our newest business texts cover these issues and subjects, the workplace is for many the schoolroom for learning about and coping with the volatility of a changing job climate and workplace environment.

Business education is about content. In the course of a standard four-year business program, you've been exposed to marketing, economics, management principles, accounting, and organizational behavior. You'll need all of this information. But one area your studies will not explore is how you make your way from the graduation platform into a job that is designed to fit your education and preparation. And today, more than ever, that journey from classroom to employer is more challenging, more competitive, and less predictable than ever before.

Just look in yesterday's newspaper or at tonight's network news and you will see examples of the way things are changing. Large financial institutions are merging into mega-sized financial institutions. Hospital corporations join to form comprehensive medical-care networks. Smaller colleges become subsumed into larger university organizations. As part of merging, redundancies in positions occur and large numbers (often thousands) of employees lose their jobs. Most of these job losses affect the middle-management level of employee—college-educated business majors. As a new college graduate, you need to keep in mind that you are in competition for jobs with these folks.

Plotting a Course for Success

It's easy to be discouraged. You need to remember that one of the best ways to succeed is to anticipate problems and design a strategy for success. If you're determined to surmount these challenges, you'll appreciate the following tips:

Don't Rest on Your Major

One of the most important and continuing changes in the business world today is the trimming down of staff size. Organizations are becoming leaner, and each employee is expected to wear many hats and have diverse skills. Certainly in organizations experiencing a downsizing or merger, the employees who survive personnel cuts most likely are those who can offer the most talent to the firm.

Choosing a marketing, or management, or economics major has put you on a certain educational path. Marketing majors usually only have the basic accounting courses. Management majors may take more math courses than marketing majors. Economics majors certainly receive more economic theory than accounting students. Sometimes, certain business majors are selected to avoid certain courses that are perceived as more difficult. But your required curriculum will not serve as an excuse to an employer who needs you to know more than a little bit about each of these areas.

College has all this knowledge and training available in one location. You won't have that luxury again. Take advantage of it, and don't assume your major is a complete meal ticket. Sample other areas of business, and become a well-rounded business student, not just a declared major!

Strengthen Your Achilles' Heel

We all have weak spots—areas we feel less than confident about in our abilities. For some, it may be statistics; for others, the analytical skills demanded in interpreting an annual report; for still others, grasping the macroeconomic concepts necessary to make sense of forecasts of Gross National Product, the stock market, or the balance of international trade.

Every addition to today's leaner workforce comes under intense scrutiny and is competing for that position not only with other recent college graduates but with scores of older, more experienced workers as well. You'll feel better about yourself and stronger as a contender if you take steps now, while you're in college, to address these gaps in your education. For those areas in which you are weak, take a general course, ask a professor to recommend some good reading, or seek tutorial assistance from a senior-level student.

Do whatever it takes to avoid finding yourself in a situation someday where you'd need to apologize for your ignorance.

Use the Classroom as Your Training Ground

Reading this book is one indication you want to be prepared for the job search. You realize it's going to be rough, and you want to be ready. But the job search is really only the first step in testing your intellectual and personal skills. These days, the job itself can be a continuing exercise in thinking creatively, overcoming challenges, and responding positively to adverse conditions. As Oscar Wilde said, "In this world there are only two tragedies. One is not getting what one wanted, and the other is getting it."

Wilde realized that we often put so much emphasis on our desire for something that we fail to think carefully about holding on to it. You can't breathe easier once you've got your job. You need to keep learning, meeting deadlines, and improving your performance so you remain a valuable employee, deserving of increased responsibility and trust and pay.

Don't wait until the rigors of the job search are staring you in the face. You have the best practice conditions available to you right now. How many of us have sat passively in the classroom, missing opportunity after opportunity to test our thinking, to learn to get our information right, and to present our arguments? Class participation is a superb beginning for the give-and-take of the world of business. It will teach you to think before you speak, respond evenly and calmly to challenges to your thinking, and to listen to and appreciate the ideas of others. Taking advantage of these classroom opportunities for personal growth may be one of the easiest and yet most important steps you could take to ensure job success!

Treat your teachers as your bosses. Practice your interaction. Ask questions and clarify instructions. Stop by their offices and get to know them outside the classroom. Try and grasp their philosophy of teaching. Let them get to know you. It's good practice for supervisor/employee relations. Such interaction also creates a good basis for letters of reference.

Treat fellow students as colleagues or fellow employees. Make contact with your classmates. Practice and refine your social skills. Your classmates are similar to some of the people you'll be working alongside, and you have a perfect opportunity to develop ease and confidence meeting and learning from all the people who populate your classrooms. Take any group work seriously and realize that any difficulties concerning meeting times, assignments, or leadership roles aren't any different than those you'll encounter on the job. Practice your group skills and contributions now in class for real success in work groups later.

Meet Businesspeople

Don't let your job interviews be your first serious contact with businesspeople. Make the most of your business faculty and their contacts and your career office with its database of alumni in order to meet businesspeople while you're studying business. There are many solid reasons why meeting practicing business professionals during your college years is a smart move. You can meet men and women of all ages and backgrounds with a variety of experience, and many will be willing to share that experience. You'll have a chance to appreciate the diversity present in the world of business and possibly discover some new role models for your own career plans.

By All Means, Do an Internship

There's no question that an internship is easier said than done. Most are unpaid, and that presents real challenges with the high cost of college today. Many students simply feel they cannot afford to not work for pay during the summer or other breaks from school. Think about this, however: giving up some income now can pay real dividends at graduation time. Many, many internships turn into real jobs for graduates. For others, the internship gives them deeper, more concrete insights into their own skills and an appreciation of the roles they can play in an organization. They are apt to find it easier to relate to people interviewing them, they have more to say, and, as a result of their internship, more to offer. They get hired!

Internships often require a relocation. If you live in a rural area or go to college in a nonmetropolitan area, nearby internships will be scarce. The greatest concentrations of internships tend to be in and around metropolitan areas where there are more organizations that can afford to train temporary, nonpaid additions to their staffs and provide meaningful work for them. You may have to seek the hospitality of a relative or one of your parent's friends or even seek inexpensive temporary housing in order to put yourself where the internships are located. The payoff still applies.

Finding and applying for internships is a monumental task, though not as difficult as finding your first job. Not all good internships are published in directories. Information on some arrive in your business department or career office on broadsheets. Check with both places as well as at your college library. Expect to write many, many cover letters and mail them out with your résumé, and be sure to do it early. Many summer internships have January or February application deadlines.

Expect to receive requests for transcripts (both official and unofficial) or requests to complete formal applications that may include essay writing about your intent or goals. All of this correspondence must be perfect, because in most cases, interns are chosen on the basis of the written materials submitted as well as phone interviews. Your written work makes your first impression.

The competitiveness of internships today is good practice and mirrors the competitiveness of the job market in general. Books such as *Internships 96* and *The 100 Best Internships* detail the previous year's competition. Some internships receive five hundred applications for three or four available internship spots.

Expect a well-chosen internship experience to stay with you for the rest of your life. That summer or term in an advertising agency, public relations firm, corporate office, government agency, or industrial site will stay with you and become part of your experiential base as long as you are in business. Internships represent a smart move for your future.

Setting Sail for a Bright Future

We've examined how business has changed and continues to change and the implications of that for you as a business major.

You now understand the responsibility you have to make the most of your remaining college years, and you have some specific techniques to use for that. Some people say college isn't the real world and you can float along, just treading water. I guarantee if you get out and meet some recent alumni of your school, they will assure you that college has the potential for being as real a world as you want to make it and that it can be an important aspect of your preparation for a business career.

Perhaps you are reading this as a junior or even a senior approaching graduation. Your most important goal right now is determining a strategy for finding that job. How do you go about that, considering all you've learned about the changing climate of business?

Realize you'll have many careers and plan for that. You've seen all the warning signs that, regardless of how talented you are, shifts in employers and employee bases do occur and some people must move on. Those that have the least trouble moving do the following things.

Watch Trends

If you're in advertising and you see an increasing use of CD-ROM and interactive advertising on computer, it's a clear sign not only that you need to be developing some skills in that area but that future growth will probably occur in firms that produce those kinds of products and materials. Stay abreast of changes in your field so you have some ready reference points if you do need to jump-start your career.

Understand Your Needs

Every time we make a job change, we have to address issues such as geographic location, housing options, pay levels, duties and responsibilities, our interest and belief in the nature of the work, our consumption patterns, and a thousand other issues that profoundly impact who we are and how we live. Begin to appreciate and understand what you need and what is important to you. That will make job choices and job shifts easier.

As a college career counselor who sees many adult alumni clients, I am too familiar with the economic realities of the job search. The most common laments I hear are "I haven't saved enough money to make a job change" and "I have so much debt I can't afford to take any less with a new job, no matter how great that new job is." These are sad comments on a situation that is easily remedied by reducing consumption and increasing savings.

It is wise to keep your needs as simple as possible and to make financial security one of your goals, for any number of reasons.

Stay Alert to the Difference Between Contextual and Portable Skills

Contextual skills are those understandings, techniques, vocabularies, relationships, and factors directly related to your business but of little value outside your field of work. Portable skills are the talents, knowledge, and techniques that can move from job to job. You need both to succeed, but you want to pay attention to the balance.

For example, if you're doing fund-raising for a major conservation group, everything you know about wetlands preservation, federal legislation to preserve wildlife habitats, public access to wetlands, and influential people in the conservation movement is part of your contextual base for expertise in this area. You can't raise money and talk authoritatively to potential donors unless you know this context and know it well. However, if you lose your job for whatever reason, unless you stay in conservation, it will not be these contextual skills that are important, it will be the portable skills.

The portable skills are your fund-raising ability, your ability to do special-event planning and promotion, your publicity and public relations talents, your "friend-raising" techniques and success stories, your ability to direct volunteer efforts and provide meaningful work assignments for volunteers, your talent at creating attractive brochures, letters, and other public communications, and your presentation skills. These talents and techniques are those that you will carry from job to job, no matter what the particular context of each job.

Pay attention to what you're learning on the job, and maintain a good balance between context and portability. If your firm is offering training in database management, you might not think of taking advantage of it because you aren't currently using databases. However, this kind of training is a portable skill and may be a valuable credential on your résumé at some future point. Take advantage of your firm's training opportunities and add to your portable skills. You'll be a more talented employee and a more viable job applicant in the future.

PART ONE

THE JOB SEARCH

1

The Self-Assessment

Self-assessment is the process by which you begin to acknowledge your own particular blend of education, experiences, values, needs, and goals. It provides the foundation for career planning and the entire job search process. Self-assessment involves looking inward and asking yourself what can sometimes prove to be difficult questions. This self-examination should lead to an intimate understanding of your personal traits, your personal values, your consumption patterns and economic needs, your longer-term goals, your skill base, your preferred skills, and your underdeveloped skills.

You come to the self-assessment process knowing yourself well in some of these areas, but you may still be uncertain about other aspects. You may be well aware of your consumption patterns, but have you spent much time specifically identifying your longer-term goals or your personal values as they relate to work? No matter what level of self-assessment you have undertaken to date, it is now time to clarify all of these issues and questions as they relate to the job search.

The knowledge you gain in the self-assessment process will guide the rest of your job search. In this book, you will learn about all of the following tasks:

- Writing résumés and cover letters
- Researching careers and networking
- Interviewing and job offer considerations

In each of these steps, you will rely on and often return to the understanding gained through your self-assessment. Any individual seeking employment must be able and willing to express these facets of his or her personality to recruiters and interviewers throughout the job search. This communication allows you to show the world who you are so that together with employers you can determine whether there will be a workable match with a given job or career path.

How to Conduct a Self-Assessment

The self-assessment process goes on naturally all the time. People ask you to clarify what you mean, you make a purchasing decision, or you begin a new relationship. You react to the world and the world reacts to you. How you understand these interactions and any changes you might make because of them are part of the natural process of self-discovery. There is, however, a more comprehensive and efficient way to approach self-assessment with regard to employment.

Because self-assessment can become a complex exercise, we have distilled it into a seven-step process that provides an effective basis for undertaking a job search. The seven steps include the following:

1. Understanding your personal traits
2. Identifying your personal values
3. Calculating your economic needs
4. Exploring your longer-term goals
5. Enumerating your skill base
6. Recognizing your preferred skills
7. Assessing skills needing further development

As you work through your self-assessment, you might want to create a worksheet similar to the one shown in Exhibit 1.1, starting on the following page. Or you might want to keep a journal of the thoughts you have as you undergo this process. There will be many opportunities to revise your self-assessment as you start down the path of seeking a career.

Step 1 Understanding Your Personal Traits
Each person has a unique personality that he or she brings to the job search process. Gaining a better understanding of your personal traits can help you evaluate job and career choices. Identifying these traits and then finding employment that allows you to draw on at least some of them can create a rewarding and fulfilling work experience. If potential employment doesn't allow you to use these preferred traits, it is important to decide whether you

Exhibit 1.1
SELF-ASSESSMENT WORKSHEET

Step 1. Understand Your Personal Traits
The personal traits that describe me are:
(Include all of the words that describe you.)
The ten personal traits that most accurately describe me are:
(List these ten traits.)

Step 2. Identify Your Personal Values
Working conditions that are important to me include:
(List working conditions that would have to exist for you to accept a position.)
The values that go along with my working conditions are:
(Write down the values that correspond to each working condition.)
Some additional values I've decided to include are:
(List those values you identify as you conduct this job search.)

Step 3. Calculate Your Economic Needs
My estimated minimum annual salary requirement is:
(Write the salary you have calculated based on your budget.)
Starting salaries for the positions I'm considering are:
(List the name of each job you are considering and the associated starting salary.)

Step 4. Explore Your Longer-Term Goals
My thoughts on longer-term goals right now are:
(Jot down some of your longer-term goals as you know them right now.)

Step 5. Enumerate Your Skill Base
The general skills I possess are:
(List the skills that underlie tasks you are able to complete.)
The specific skills I possess are:
(List more technical or specific skills that you possess, and indicate your level of expertise.)
General and specific skills that I want to promote to employers for the jobs I'm considering are:
(List general and specific skills for each type of job you are considering.)

continued

Step 6. Recognize Your Preferred Skills

Skills that I would like to use on the job include:

(List skills that you hope to use on the job, and indicate how often you'd like to use them.)

Step 7. Assess Skills Needing Further Development

Some skills that I'll need to acquire for the jobs I'm considering include:

(Write down skills listed in job advertisements or job descriptions that you don't currently possess.)

I believe I can build these skills by:

(Describe how you plan to acquire these skills.)

can find other ways to express them or whether you would be better off not considering this type of job. Interests and hobbies pursued outside of work hours can be one way to use personal traits you don't have an opportunity to draw on in your work. For example, if you consider yourself an outgoing person and the kinds of jobs you are examining allow little contact with other people, you may be able to achieve the level of interaction that is comfortable for you outside of your work setting. If such a compromise seems impractical or otherwise unsatisfactory, you probably should explore only jobs that provide the interaction you want and need on the job.

Many young adults who are not very confident about their employability will downplay their need for income. They will say, "Money is not all that important if I love my work." But if you begin to document exactly what you need for housing, transportation, insurance, clothing, food, and utilities, you will begin to understand that some jobs cannot meet your financial needs and it doesn't matter how wonderful the job is. If you have to worry each payday about bills and other financial obligations, you won't be very effective on the job. Begin now to be honest with yourself about your needs.

Begin the self-assessment process by creating an inventory of your personal traits. Make a list of as many words as possible to describe yourself. Words like *accurate, creative, future-oriented, relaxed,* or *structured* are just a few examples. In addition, you might ask people who know you well how they might describe you.

Focusing on Selected Personal Traits. Of all the traits you identified, select the ten you believe most accurately describe you. Keep track of these ten traits.

Considering Your Personal Traits in the Job Search Process. As you begin exploring jobs and careers, watch for matches between your personal traits and the job descriptions you read. Some jobs will require many personal traits you know you possess, and others will not seem to match those traits.

Working in sales, for example, will draw upon your reserves of creativity, poise, and sociability. Sales is essentially problem solving, not persuasion. Your ability to listen attentively, analyze problems, and prescribe solutions will be far more important personal traits for success than fast-talking and pressure tactics. Sales positions for business graduates often require the mastery of sophisticated product information. Attention to detail and memory are also important attributes for this work.

Your ability to respond to changing conditions, your decision-making ability, productivity, creativity, and verbal skills all have a bearing on your success in and enjoyment of your work life. To better guarantee success, be sure to take the time needed to understand these traits in yourself.

Step 2   Identifying Your Personal Values

Your personal values affect every aspect of your life, including employment, and they develop and change as you move through life. Values can be defined as principles that we hold in high regard, qualities that are important and desirable to us. Some values aren't ordinarily connected to work (love, beauty, color, light, relationships, family, or religion), and others are (autonomy, cooperation, effectiveness, achievement, knowledge, and security). Our values determine, in part, the level of satisfaction we feel in a particular job.

Defining Acceptable Working Conditions. One facet of employment is the set of working conditions that must exist for someone to consider taking a job.

Each of us would probably create a unique list of acceptable working conditions, but items that might be included on many people's lists are the amount of money you would need to be paid, how far you are willing to drive or travel, the amount of freedom you want in determining your own schedule, whether you would be working with people or data or things, and the types of tasks you would be willing to do. Your conditions might include statements of working conditions you will *not* accept; for example, you might not be willing to work at night or on weekends or holidays.

If you were offered a job tomorrow, what conditions would have to exist for you to realistically consider accepting the position? Take some time and make a list of these conditions.

Realizing Associated Values. Your list of working conditions can be used to create an inventory of your values relating to jobs and careers you are exploring. For example, if one of your conditions stated that you wanted to earn at least $30,000 per year, the associated value would be financial gain. If another condition was that you wanted to work with a friendly group of people, the value that went along with that might be belonging or interaction with people.

Relating Your Values to the World of Work. As you read the job descriptions you come across either in this book, in newspapers and magazines, or online, think about the values associated with each position.

For example, in sales, your duties may include calling on clients, explaining products and/or services you offer, arranging delivery, and/or installing and providing follow-up services after the sale.

At least some of the associated values in the field you're exploring should match those you extracted from your list of working conditions. Take a second look at any values that don't match up. How important are they to you? What will happen if they are not satisfied on the job? Can you incorporate those personal values elsewhere? Your answers need to be brutally honest. As you continue your exploration, be sure to add to your list any additional values that occur to you.

Step 3 Calculating Your Economic Needs
Each of us grew up in an environment that provided for certain basic needs, such as food and shelter, and, to varying degrees, other needs that we now consider basic, such as cable television, E-mail, or an automobile. Needs such as privacy, space, and quiet, which at first glance may not appear to be monetary needs, may add to housing expenses and so should be considered as you examine your economic needs. For example, if you place a high value on a large, open living space for yourself, it would be difficult to satisfy that need without an associated high housing cost, especially in a densely populated city environment.

As you prepare to move into the world of work and become responsible for meeting your own basic needs, it is important to consider the salary you will need to be able to afford a satisfying standard of living. The three-step process outlined here will help you plan a budget, which in turn will allow you to evaluate the various career choices and geographic locations you are considering. The steps include (1) developing a realistic budget, (2) examining starting salaries, and (3) using a cost-of-living index.

Developing a Realistic Budget. Each of us has certain expectations for the kind of lifestyle we want to maintain. To begin the process of defining your economic needs, it will be helpful to determine what you expect to spend on routine monthly expenses. These expenses include housing, food, transportation, entertainment, utilities, loan repayments, and revolving charge accounts. You may not currently spend anything for certain items, but you probably will have to once you begin supporting yourself. As you develop this budget, be generous in your estimates, but keep in mind any items that could be reduced or eliminated. If you are not sure about the cost of a certain item, talk with family or friends who would be able to give you a realistic estimate.

If this is new or difficult for you, start to keep a log of expenses right now. You may be surprised at how much you actually spend each month for food or stamps or magazines. Household expenses and personal grooming items can often loom very large in a budget, as can auto repairs or home maintenance.

Income taxes must also be taken into consideration when examining salary requirements. State and local taxes vary, so it is difficult to calculate exactly the effect of taxes on the amount of income you need to generate. To roughly estimate the gross income necessary to generate your minimum annual salary requirement, multiply the minimum salary you have calculated by a factor of 1.35. The resulting figure will be an approximation of what your gross income would need to be, given your estimated expenses.

Examining Starting Salaries. Starting salaries for each of the career tracks are provided throughout this book. These salary figures can be used in conjunction with the cost-of-living index (discussed in the next section) to determine whether you would be able to meet your basic economic needs in a given geographic location.

Using a Cost-of-Living Index. If you are thinking about trying to get a job in a geographic region other than the one where you now live, understanding differences in the cost of living will help you come to a more informed decision about making a move. By using a cost-of-living index, you can compare salaries offered and the cost of living in different locations with what you know about the salaries offered and the cost of living in your present location.

Many variables are used to calculate the cost-of-living index. Often included are housing, groceries, utilities, transportation, health care, clothing, and entertainment expenses. Right now you do not need to worry about the details associated with calculating a given index. The main purpose of this exercise is to help you understand that pay ranges for entry-level positions may not vary greatly, but the cost of living in different locations *can* vary tremendously.

If you lived in Cleveland, Ohio, for example, and you were interested in working as a sales representative for a consumer goods firm, you would earn, on average, $25,390 annually. But let's say you're also thinking about moving to either New York, Los Angeles, or Denver. You know you can live on $25,390 in Cleveland, but you want to be able to equal that salary in other locations you're considering. How much will you need to earn in those locations to do this? Figuring the cost of living for each city will show you.

Let's walk through this example. In any cost-of-living index, the number 100 represents the national average cost of living, and each city is assigned an index number based on current prices in that city for the items included in the index (housing, food, etc.). In the index we used, New York was assigned the number 177.0, Los Angeles's index was 137.2, Denver's was 104.7, and Cleveland's index was 103.9. We can set up a table to determine exactly how much you would have to earn in each of these cities to have the same buying power that you have in Cleveland. (Many websites now offer calculators to help you do this; our index is taken from the American Chamber of Commerce Researchers Association's latest [2002] compilation of comparative costs of living.)

You would have to earn $43,253 in New York, $33,528 in Los Angeles, and $25,586 in Denver to match the buying power of $25,390 in Cleveland.

JOB: SALES REPRESENTATIVE

City	Index	Base	Equivalent Salary
New York	177.0		
		× $25,390 = $43,253	
Cleveland	103.9		

Los Angeles	137.2		
		× $25,390 = $33,528	
Cleveland	103.9		

Denver	104.7		
		× $25,390 = $25,586	
Cleveland	103.9		

Index is the American Chamber of Commerce Researchers Association cost-of-living index found at accra.org.
Base is Cleveland sales representative average entry-level salary.
Source: BLS 2000 Metropolitan Area Occupational Employment Salary Estimates.

If you would like to determine whether it's financially worthwhile to make any of these moves, one more piece of information is needed: the salaries of sales representatives in these other cities. The Bureau of Labor Statistics Occupational Employment and Salary data (2000) is the source we used. Another source is American Salaries and Wages Survey (6th ed., Detroit: Gale Group, 2001).

Region	Annual Salary	Salary Equivalent to Ohio	Change in Buying Power
Mid-Atlantic (including New York)	$24,390	$43,253	−$18,863
West (including Los Angeles)	$20,580	$33,527	−$12,947
Mountain Plains (including Denver)	$25,490	$25,585	−$95

Source: Bureau of Labor Statistics, 2000 Occupational Employment and Salary data files.

> If you moved to New York City and secured employment as a sales representative in the wholesale or manufacturing sector, you would not be able to maintain a lifestyle similar to the one you led in Cleveland; in fact, you would almost have to double your income to maintain a similar lifestyle in New York. The situation is a bit better in Los Angeles, and you could expect to just about break even on a lateral move to Denver. Using other cities, you would probably find somewhere you would actually increase your buying power. But, of course, you should factor in the long-term career opportunities that come from moving to one of these major cities.

You can work through a similar exercise for any type of job you are considering and for many locations when current salary information is available. It will be worth your time to undertake this analysis if you are seriously considering a relocation. By doing so you will be able to make an informed choice.

Step 4 Exploring Your Longer-Term Goals

There is no question that when we first begin working, our goals are to use our skills and education in a job that will reward us with employment, income, and status relative to the preparation we brought with us to this position. If we are not being paid as much as we feel we should for our level of education or if job demands don't provide the intellectual stimulation we had hoped for, we experience unhappiness and as a result often seek other employment.

Most jobs we consider "good" are those that fulfill our basic "lower-level" needs of security, food, clothing, shelter, income, and productive work. But even when our basic needs are met and our jobs are secure and productive, we as individuals are constantly changing. As we change, the demands and expectations we place on our jobs may change. Fortunately, some jobs grow and change with us, and this explains why some people are happy throughout many years in a job.

But more often people are bigger than the jobs they fill. We have more goals and needs than any job could satisfy. These are "higher-level" needs of self-esteem, companionship, affection, and an increasing desire to feel we are employing ourselves in the most effective way possible. Not all of these higher-level needs can be met through employment, but for as long as we are employed, we increasingly demand that our jobs play their part in moving us along the path to fulfillment.

Another obvious but important fact is that we change as we mature. Although our jobs also have the potential for change, they may not change as frequently or as markedly as we do. There are increasingly fewer one-job, one-employer careers; we must think about a work future that may involve voluntary or forced moves from employer to employer. Because of that very real possibility, we need to take advantage of the opportunities in each position we hold. Acquiring the skills and competencies associated with each position will keep us viable and attractive as employees. This is particularly true in a job market that not only is technology/computer dependent, but also is populated with more and more small, self-transforming organizations rather than the large, seemingly stable organizations of the past.

If you are considering a position in retailing, you would gain a better perspective on this career if you could talk to an entry-level associate buyer, a more senior and experienced department head or branch store manager, and finally, a vice president for sales merchandising or store operations who has a considerable work history in the retail sector. Each will have a different perspective, unique concerns, and an individual set of value priorities.

Step 5 Enumerating Your Skill Base

In terms of the job search, skills can be thought of as capabilities that can be developed in school, at work, or by volunteering and then used in specific job settings. Many studies have documented the kinds of skills that employers seek in entry-level applicants. For example, some of the most desired skills for individuals interested in the teaching profession are the ability to interact effectively with students one-on-one, to manage a classroom, to adapt to varying situations as necessary, and to get involved in school activities. Business employers have also identified important qualities, including enthusiasm for the employer's product or service, a businesslike mind, the ability to follow written or oral instructions, the ability to demonstrate self-control, the confidence to suggest new ideas, the ability to communicate with all members of a group, an awareness of cultural differences, and loyalty, to name just a few. You will find that many of these skills are also in the repertoire of qualities demanded in your college major.

To be successful in obtaining any given job, you must be able to demonstrate that you possess a certain mix of skills that will allow you to carry out the duties required by that job. This skill mix will vary a great deal from job to job; to determine the skills necessary for the jobs you are seeking, you can read job advertisements or more generic job descriptions, such as those found later in this book. If you want to be effective in the job search, you must directly show employers that you possess the skills needed to be successful in filling the position. These skills will initially be described on your résumé and then discussed again during the interview process.

Skills are either general or specific. To develop a list of skills relevant to employers, you must first identify the general skills you possess, then list specific skills you have to offer, and, finally, examine which of these skills employers are seeking.

Identifying Your General Skills. Because you possess or will possess a college degree, employers will assume that you can read and write, perform certain basic computations, think critically, and communicate effectively. Employers will want to see that you have acquired these skills, and they will want to know which additional general skills you possess.

One way to begin identifying skills is to write an experiential diary. An experiential diary lists all the tasks you were responsible for completing for each job you've held and then outlines the skills required to do those tasks. You may list several skills for any given task. This diary allows you to distinguish between the tasks you performed and the underlying skills required to complete those tasks. Here's an example:

Tasks	Skills
Answering telephone	Effective use of language, clear diction, ability to direct inquiries, ability to solve problems
Waiting on tables	Poise under conditions of time and pressure, speed, accuracy, good memory, simultaneous completion of tasks, sales skills

For each job or experience you have participated in, develop a worksheet based on the example shown here. On a résumé, you may want to describe these skills rather than simply listing tasks. Skills are easier for the employer to appreciate, especially when your experience is very different from the employment you are seeking. In addition to helping you identify general skills, this experiential diary will prepare you to speak more effectively in an interview about the qualifications you possess.

Identifying Your Specific Skills. It may be easier to identify your specific skills because you can definitely say whether you can speak other languages, program a computer, draft a map or diagram, or edit a document using appropriate symbols and terminology.

Using your experiential diary, identify the points in your history where you learned how to do something very specific, and decide whether you have a beginning, intermediate, or advanced knowledge of how to use that particular skill. Right now, be sure to list *every* specific skill you have, and don't consider whether you like using the skill. Write down a list of specific skills you have acquired and the level of competence you possess—beginning, intermediate, or advanced.

Relating Your Skills to Employers. You probably have thought about a couple of different jobs you might be interested in obtaining, and one way to begin relating the general and specific skills you possess to a potential employer's needs is to read actual advertisements for these types of positions (see Part Two for resources listing actual job openings).

For example, you might be interested in working as a financial analyst for an investment banking firm, prior to returning to graduate school for your M.B.A. (Master's in Business Administration). A typical job listing might read, "Conduct financial analysis, economic evaluations, and profitability studies pertaining to new business opportunities. Bachelor's degree in business and excellent PC skills required. Experience with venture financing preferred." If you then used any one of a number of general sources of information that described the job of financial analyst, you would find additional information. Financial analysts also track and report on competitive information, manage multiple projects simultaneously, interpret financial data, and advise management about trends.

Begin building a comprehensive list of required skills with the first job description you read. Exploring advertisements for and descriptions of several types of related positions will reveal an important core of skills that are necessary for obtaining the type of work you're interested in. In building this list, include both general and specific skills.

Following is a sample list of skills needed to be successful as a financial analyst in investment banking. These items were extracted from general resources and actual job listings.

JOB: FINANCIAL ANALYST/
INVESTMENT BANKING

General Skills	Specific Skills
Accounting	Estimating company worth
Reading	Tracking market data
Gathering information	Analyzing income statements
Decision making	Evaluating alternatives
Meeting deadlines	Generating color graphics
Attending meetings	Using annual reports
Collaborating on projects	Generating ratios
Entering data into computer	Mastering various software packages
Writing	Editing presentations

On separate sheets of paper, try to generate a comprehensive list of required skills for at least one of the jobs you are considering.

The list of general skills that you develop for a given career path would be valuable for any number of jobs you might apply for. Many of the specific skills would also be transferable to other types of positions. For example, tracking market data is a required skill for market analysts, consultants, and product managers, and would be helpful for marketing managers as well.

Now review the list of skills that are required for jobs you are considering, and check off those skills that *you know you possess*. You should refer to these specific skills on the résumé that you write for this type of job. See Chapter 2 for details on résumé writing.

Step 6   Recognizing Your Preferred Skills

In the previous section you developed a comprehensive list of skills that relate to particular career paths that are of interest to you. You can now relate these to skills that you prefer to use. We all use a wide range of skills (some researchers say individuals have a repertoire of about five hundred skills), but we may not particularly be interested in using all of them in our work. There may be some skills that come to us more naturally or that we use successfully time and time again and that we want to continue to use; these are best described as our preferred skills. For this exercise use the list of skills that you created for the previous section, and decide which of them you are *most interested in using* in future work and how often you would like to use them. You might be interested in using some skills only occasionally, while others you would like to use more regularly. You probably also have skills that you hope you can use constantly.

As you examine job announcements, look for matches between this list of preferred skills and the qualifications described in the advertisements. These skills should be highlighted on your résumé and discussed in job interviews.

Step 7   Assessing Skills Needing Further Development

Previously you compiled a list of general and specific skills required for given positions. You already possess some of these skills; those that remain to be developed are your underdeveloped skills.

If you are just beginning the job search, there may be gaps between the qualifications required for some of the jobs you're considering and the skills you possess. The thought of having to admit to and talk about these underdeveloped skills, especially in a job interview, is a frightening one. One way to put a healthy perspective on this subject is to target and relate your exploration of underdeveloped skills to the types of positions you are seeking. Recognizing these shortcomings and planning to overcome them with either on-the-job training or additional formal education can be a positive way to address the concept of underdeveloped skills.

On your worksheet or in your journal, make a list of up to five general or specific skills required for the positions you're interested in that you *don't currently possess*. For each item list an idea you have for specific action you could take to acquire that skill. Do some brainstorming to come up with possible actions. If you have a hard time generating ideas, talk to people currently working in this type of position, professionals in your college career services office, trusted friends, family members, or members of related professional associations.

In the chapter on interviewing, we will discuss in detail how to effectively address questions about underdeveloped skills. Generally speaking, though, employers want genuine answers to these types of questions. They want you to reveal "the real you," and they also want to see how you answer difficult questions. In taking the positive, targeted approach discussed above, you show the employer that you are willing to continue to learn and that you have a plan for strengthening your job qualifications.

Using Your Self-Assessment

Exploring entry-level career options can be an exciting experience if you have good resources available and will take the time to use them. Can you effectively complete the following tasks?

1. Understand your personality traits and relate them to career choices
2. Define your personal values
3. Determine your economic needs
4. Explore longer-term goals
5. Understand your skill base
6. Recognize your preferred skills
7. Express a willingness to improve on your underdeveloped skills

If so, then you can more meaningfully participate in the job search process by writing a more effective résumé, finding job titles that represent work you are interested in doing, locating job sites that will provide the opportunity for you to use your strengths and skills, networking in an informed way, participating in focused interviews, getting the most out of follow-up contacts, and evaluating job offers to find those that create a good match between you and the employer. The remaining chapters in Part One guide you through these next steps in the job search process. For many job seekers, this process can take anywhere from three months to a year to implement. The time you will need to put into your job search will depend on the type of job you want and the geographic location where you'd like to work. Think of your effort as a job in itself, requiring you to set aside time each week to complete the needed work. Carefully undertaken efforts may reduce the time you need for your job search.

2

The Résumé and Cover Letter

The task of writing a résumé may seem overwhelming if you are unfamiliar with this type of document, but there are some easily understood techniques that can and should be used. This section was written to help you understand the purpose of the résumé, the different types of résumé formats available, and how to write the sections of information traditionally found on a résumé. We will present examples and explanations that address questions frequently posed by people writing their first résumé or updating an old résumé.

Even within the formats and suggestions given, however, there are infinite variations. True, most résumés follow one of the outlines suggested, but you should feel free to adjust the résumé to suit your needs and make it expressive of your life and experience.

Why Write a Résumé?

The purpose of a résumé is to convince an employer that you should be interviewed. Whether you're mailing, faxing, or E-mailing this document, you'll want to present enough information to show that you can make an immediate and valuable contribution to an organization. A résumé is not an in-depth historical or legal document; later in the job search process you may be asked to document your entire work history on an application form and attest to its validity. The résumé should, instead, highlight relevant information pertaining directly to the organization that will receive the document or to the type of position you are seeking.

We will discuss the chronological and digital résumés in detail here. Functional and targeted résumés, which are used much less often, are briefly discussed. The reasons for using one type of résumé over another and the typical format for each are addressed in the following sections.

The Chronological Résumé

The chronological résumé is the most common of the various résumé formats and therefore the format that employers are most used to receiving. This type of résumé is easy to read and understand because it details the chronological progression of jobs you have held. (See Exhibit 2.1.) It begins with your most recent employment and works back in time. If you have a solid work history or have experience that provided growth and development in your duties and responsibilities, a chronological résumé will highlight these achievements. The typical elements of a chronological résumé include the heading, a career objective, educational background, employment experience, activities, and references.

The Heading
The heading consists of your name, address, telephone number, and other means of contact. This may include a fax number, E-mail address, and your home-page address. If you are using a shared E-mail account or a parent's business fax, be sure to let others who use these systems know that you may receive important professional correspondence via these systems. You wouldn't want to miss a vital E-mail or fax! Likewise, if your résumé directs readers to a personal home page on the Web, be certain it's a professional personal home page designed to be viewed and appreciated by a prospective employer. This may mean making substantial changes in the home page you currently mount on the Web.

The Objective. Without a doubt the objective statement is the most challenging part of the résumé for most writers. Even for individuals who have decided on a career path, it can be difficult to encapsulate all they want to say in one or two brief sentences. For job seekers who are unfocused or unclear about their intentions, trying to write this section can inhibit the entire résumé writing process.

Keep the objective as short as possible and no longer than two short sentences.

Exhibit 2.1
CHRONOLOGICAL RÉSUMÉ

MARIANNE FLAMAND

Duchess Hall #801	2068 Lincoln
Indiana University	Montreal, P.Q.
Bloomington, IN 01234	H3H 1H9
(317) 555-1234	Canada
(until May 2002)	(514) 555-6798

OBJECTIVE

Entry-level position in health-care administration. Special interest in managed care sales and contracting.

EDUCATION

Bachelor of Science Degree in Business Management
Indiana University, Bloomington, Indiana, May 2002
Concentration: Human Resources Management
Minor: Psychology

EXPERIENCE

<u>Intern.</u> Humana Hospital Corporation, August, GA, Summer 2001
A rotating internship throughout the corporate office divisions, including human resources, marketing, strategic planning, accounting, and finance. Portfolio of projects completed during the internship available upon request.

<u>Staff.</u> Admission, Discharge and Transfer Services, Westwood Hospital, Montreal, Canada, Summers 1999–2000
Increasing responsibility in this busy department of a 250-bed general hospital assisting in the administration of admission and discharge services. Extensive information systems experience. No patient contact in this position.

<u>Line Cook.</u> KiWi Kitchen, Burlington, VT, Summer 1998
Short-order cook for popular breakfast and lunch eatery catering to the upscale market. Emphasis on high-quality, well-presented meals. Attention to detail, portion control critical.

continued

COMMUNITY SERVICE
Volunteer, Medical Records Department, Spear Hospital, Spear, IN
Intake Processor, Student Red Cross Blood Drive (three years)
Indiana University

REFERENCES
A selection of both personal and professional references are available upon
request.

Choose one of the following types of objective statement:

1. General Objective Statement

- An entry-level educational programming coordinator position

2. Position-Focused Objective

- To obtain the position of conference coordinator at State College

3. Industry-Focused Objective

- To begin a career as a sales representative in the cruise line industry

4. Summary of Qualifications Statement

A degree in business and four years of progressively increasing
job responsibility in the telecommunications industry have prepared me to begin a career as a computer analyst with a pro-
priety security firm that values hard work and dedication.

Support Your Objective. A résumé that contains any one of these types
of objective statements should then go on to demonstrate why you are qualified to get the position. Listing academic degrees can be one way to indicate qualifications. Another demonstration would be in the way previous
experiences, both volunteer and paid, are described. Without this kind of doc-

umentation in the body of the résumé, the objective looks unsupported. Think of the résumé as telling a connected story about you. All the elements should work together to form a coherent picture that ideally should relate to your statement of objective.

Education

This section of your résumé should indicate the exact name of the degree you will receive or have received, spelled out completely with no abbreviations. The degree is generally listed after the objective, followed by the institution name and location, and then the month and year of graduation. This section could also include your academic minor, grade point average (GPA), and appearance on the Dean's List or President's List.

If you have enough space, you might want to include a section listing courses related to the field in which you are seeking work. The best use of a "related courses" section would be to list some course work that is not traditionally associated with the major. Perhaps you took several computer courses outside your degree that will be helpful and related to the job prospects you are entertaining. Several education section examples are shown here:

- Bachelor of Science Degree in Management
  State University, Boulder, Colorado, 2002
  Concentration: Human Resource Management
- Bachelor of Science Degree in Business Management
  State College, Columbus, OH, May 2002
  Minor: Computer Science
- Bachelor of Science Degree in Management Science
  Community College, Summit, New Jersey, 2002
  General Management Option
  Minor in Economics

An example of a format for related-courses section follows:

RELATED COURSES	
Labor Management Relations	Corporate Finance
Business Computer Applications	Personnel Management
Real Estate Investment and Development	Business Research Design

---

Experience

The experience section of your résumé should be the most substantial part and should take up most of the space on the page. Employers want to see what kind of work history you have. They will look at your range of experiences, longevity in jobs, and specific tasks you are able to complete. This section may also be called "work experience," "related experience," "employment history," or "employment." No matter what you call this section, some important points to remember are the following:

1. **Describe your duties** as they relate to the position you are seeking.
2. **Emphasize major responsibilities** and indicate increases in responsibility. Include all relevant employment experiences: summer, part-time, internships, cooperative education, or self-employment.
3. **Emphasize skills**, especially those that transfer from one situation to another. The fact that you coordinated a student organization, chaired meetings, supervised others, and managed a budget leads one to suspect that you could coordinate other things as well.
4. **Use descriptive job titles** that provide information about what you did. A "Student Intern" should be more specifically stated as, for example, "Magazine Operations Intern." "Volunteer" is also too general; a title such as "Peer Writing Tutor" would be more appropriate.
5. **Create word pictures** by using active verbs to start sentences. Describe *results* you have produced in the work you have done.

A limp description would say something such as the following: "My duties included helping with production, proofreading, and editing. I used a design and page layout program." An action statement would be stated as follows: "Coordinated and assisted in the creative marketing of brochures and seminar promotions, becoming proficient in Quark."

Remember, an accomplishment is simply a result, a final measurable product that people can relate to. A duty is not a result; it is an obligation—every job holder has duties. For an effective résumé, list as many results as you can. To make the most of the limited space you have and to give your description impact, carefully select appropriate and accurate descriptors.

Here are some traits that employers tell us they like to see:

• Teamwork
• Energy and motivation

- Learning and using new skills
- Versatility
- Critical thinking
- Understanding how profits are created
- Organizational acumen
- Communicating directly and clearly, in both writing and speaking
- Risk taking
- Willingness to admit mistakes
- High personal standards

Solutions to Frequently Encountered Problems

Repetitive Employment with the Same Employer
EMPLOYMENT: The Foot Locker, Portland, Oregon. Summer 2001, 2002, 2003. Initially employed in high school as salesclerk. Due to successful performance, asked to return next two summers at higher pay with added responsibility. Ranked as the #2 salesperson the first summer and #1 the next two summers. Assisted in arranging eye-catching retail displays; served as manager of other summer workers during owner's absence.

A Large Number of Jobs
EMPLOYMENT: Recent Hospitality Industry Experience: Affiliated with four upscale hotel/restaurant complexes (September 2001–February 2004), where I worked part- and full-time as a waiter, bartender, disc jockey, and bookkeeper to produce income for college.

Several Positions with the Same Employer
EMPLOYMENT: Coca-Cola Bottling Co., Burlington, Vermont, 2001–2004. In four years, I received three promotions, each with increased pay and responsibility.

Summer Sales Coordinator: Promoted to hire, train, and direct efforts of add-on staff of fifteen college-age route salespeople hired to meet summer peak demand for product.

Sales Administrator: Promoted to run home office sales desk, managing accounts and associated delivery schedules for professional sales force of ten people. Intensive phone work, daily interaction with all personnel, and strong knowledge of product line required.

Route Salesperson: Summer employment to travel and tourism industry sites that use Coke products. Met specific schedule demands, used good communication skills with wide variety of customers, and demonstrated strong selling skills. Named salesperson of the month for July and August of that year.

Questions Résumé Writers Often Ask

How Far Back Should I Go in Terms of Listing Past Jobs?

Usually, listing three or four jobs should suffice. If you did something back in high school that has a bearing on your future aspirations for employment, by all means list the job. As you progress through your college career, high school jobs will be replaced on the résumé by college employment.

Should I Differentiate Between Paid and Nonpaid Employment?

Most employers are not initially concerned about how much you were paid. They are anxious to know how much responsibility you held in your past employment. There is no need to specify that your work was as a volunteer if you had significant responsibilities.

How Should I Represent My Accomplishments or Work-Related Responsibilities?

Succinctly, but fully. In other words, give the employer enough information to arouse curiosity but not so much detail that you leave nothing to the imagination. Besides, some jobs merit more lengthy explanations than others. Be sure to convey any information that can give an employer a better understanding of the depth of your involvement at work. Did you supervise others? How many? Did your efforts result in a more efficient operation? How much did you increase efficiency? Did you handle a budget? How much? Were you promoted in a short time? Did you work two jobs at once or fifteen hours per week after high school? Where appropriate, quantify.

Should the Work Section Always Follow the Education Section on the Résumé?

Always lead with your strengths. If your education closely relates to the employment you now seek, put this section after the objective. If your education does not closely relate but you have a surplus of good work experiences, consider reversing the order of your sections to lead with employment, followed by education.

How Should I Present My Activities, Honors, Awards, Professional Societies, and Affiliations?

This section of the résumé can add valuable information for an employer to consider if used correctly. The rule of thumb for information in this section is to include only those activities that are in some way relevant to the objective stated on your résumé. If you can draw a valid connection between your activities and your objective, include them; if not, leave them out.

Professional affiliations and honors should all be listed; especially important are those related to your job objective. Social clubs and activities need not be a part of your résumé unless you hold a significant office or you are looking for a position related to your membership. Be aware that most prospective employers' principal concerns are related to your employability, not your social life. If you have any, publications can be included as an addendum to your résumé.

How Should I Handle References?

The use of references is considered a part of the interview process, and they should never be listed on a résumé. You would always provide references to a potential employer if requested to, so it is not even necessary to include this section on the résumé if space does not permit. If space is available, it is acceptable to include the following statement:

- REFERENCES: Furnished upon request.

The Functional Résumé

The functional résumé departs from a chronological résumé in that it organizes information by specific accomplishments in various settings: previous jobs, volunteer work, associations, and so forth. This type of résumé permits you to stress the substance of your experiences rather than the position titles you have held. You should consider using a functional résumé if you have held a series of similar jobs that relied on the same skills or abilities. There are many good books in which you can find examples of functional résumés, including *How to Write a Winning Resume* or *Resumes Made Easy*.

The Targeted Résumé

The targeted résumé focuses on specific work-related capabilities you can bring to a given position within an organization. Past achievements are listed to highlight your capabilities and the work history section is abbreviated.

Digital Résumés

Today's employers have to manage an enormous number of résumés. One of the most frequent complaints the writers of this series hear from students is the failure of employers to even acknowledge the receipt of a résumé and cover letter. Frequently, the reason for this poor response or nonresponse is the volume of applications received for every job. In an attempt to better manage the considerable labor investment involved in processing large numbers of résumés, many employers are requiring digital submission of résumés. There are two types of digital résumés: those that can be E-mailed or posted to a website, called *electronic résumés*, and those that can be "read" by a computer, commonly called *scannable résumés*. Though the format may be a bit different from the traditional "paper" résumé, the goal of both types of digital résumés is the same—to get you an interview! These résumés must be designed to be "technologically friendly." What that basically means to you is that they should be free of graphics and fancy formatting. (See Exhibit 2.2.)

Electronic Résumés

Sometimes referred to as plain-text résumés, electronic résumés are designed to be E-mailed to an employer or posted to one of many commercial Internet databases such as CareerMosaic.com, America's Job Bank (ajb.dni.us), or Monster.com.

Some technical considerations:

- Electronic résumés must be written in American Standard Code for Information Interchange (ASCII), which is simply a plain-text format. These characters are universally recognized so that every computer can accurately read and understand them. To create an ASCII file of your current résumé, open your document, then save it as a text or ASCII file. This will eliminate all formatting. Edit as needed using your computer's text editor application.
- Use a standard-width typeface. Courier is a good choice because it is the font associated with ASCII in most systems.

Exhibit 2.2
DIGITAL RÉSUMÉ

ART S. MALIK   ⟵   Put your name at the top on its own line.
Current Address
Norton Bagley House
Rollins College
Winter Park, FL 78544
Phone: 914-555-2901   ⟵   Put your phone number on its own line.
E-mail: asmalik@xxx.com

Use a standard-width typeface.

Permanent Address
266 Chase Avenue
Winter Park, FL 78543
Phone: 914-555-2443

Keywords make your résumé easier to find in a database.

KEYWORD SUMMARY   ⟵
Financial Analyst, investment banking, B.S. Management

Use a space between asterisk and text.

ACHIEVEMENTS   ⟵
* Entertainment contract negotiator for College Union.
* Created student team to assist local senior citizens
with income tax preparation.
* Marketed my own line of imprinted mugs to campus
organizations.

Asterisks and plus signs replace bullets.

No line should exceed sixty-five characters.

WORK HISTORY
2000-Present (part time)
Data Analyst
Mooselake National Bank, Winter Park, FL
Using established databases, respond to a variety of
account information needs.

End each line by hitting the ENTER (or RETURN) key.

1998-2000
Student Worker, Reference Desk
Rollins College Library, Winter Park, FL
Worked with professional reference librarians to
respond to information requests from students,
faculty, staff, and townspeople.

continued

1996-1998
Recreation Leader
Winter Park Parks Department, FL
Increasing responsibilities for children's program.

EDUCATION ◄─────────────────────── Capital letters to
Bachelor of Science in Management with   emphasize headings.
Finance Option
Rollins College
Minor: English

- Use a font size of 11 to 14 points. A 12-point font is considered standard.
- Your margin should be left-justified.
- Do not exceed sixty-five characters per line because the word-wrap function doesn't operate in ASCII.
- Do not use boldface, italics, underlining, bullets, or various font sizes. Instead, use asterisks, plus signs, or all capital letters when you want to emphasize something.
- Avoid graphics and shading.
- Use as many "keywords" as you possibly can. These are words or phrases usually relating to skills or experience that either are specifically used in the job announcement or are popular buzzwords in the industry.
- Minimize abbreviations.
- Your name should be the first line of text.
- Conduct a "test run" by E-mailing your résumé to yourself and a friend before you send it to the employer. See how it transmits, and make any changes you need to. Continue to test it until it's exactly how you want it to look.
- Unless an employer specifically requests that you send the résumé in the form of an attachment, don't. Employers can encounter problems opening a document as an attachment, and there are always viruses to consider.
- Don't forget your cover letter. Send it along with your résumé as a single message.

Scannable Résumés

Some companies are relying on technology to narrow the candidate pool for available job openings. Electronic Applicant Tracking uses imaging to scan, sort, and store résumé elements in a database. Then, through OCR (Optical Character Recognition) software, the computer scans the résumés for keywords and phrases. To have the best chance at getting an interview, you want to increase the number of "hits"—matches of your skills, abilities, experience, and education to those the computer is scanning for—your résumé will get. You can see how critical using the right keywords is for this type of résumé.

Technical considerations include:

- Again, do not use boldface (newer systems may read this OK, but many older ones won't), italics, underlining, bullets, shading, graphics, or multiple font sizes. Instead, for emphasis, use asterisks, plus signs, or all capital letters. Minimize abbreviations.
- Use a popular typeface such as Courier, Helvetica, Ariel, or Palatino. Avoid decorative fonts.
- Font size should be between 11 and 14 points.
- Do not compress the spacing between letters.
- Use horizontal and vertical lines sparingly; the computer may misread them as the letters L or I.
- Left-justify the text.
- Do not use parentheses or brackets around telephone numbers, and be sure your phone number is on its own line of text.
- Your name should be the first line of text and on its own line. If your résumé is longer than one page, be sure to put your name on the top of all pages.
- Use a traditional résumé structure. The chronological format may work best.
- Use nouns that are skill-focused, such as *management, writer,* and *programming*. This is different from traditional paper résumés, which use action-oriented verbs.
- Laser printers produce the finest copies. Avoid dot-matrix printers.
- Use standard, light-colored paper with text on one side only. Since the higher the contrast, the better, your best choice is black ink on white paper.
- Always send original copies. If you must fax, set the fax on fine mode, not standard.
- Do not staple or fold your résumé. This can confuse the computer.

- Before you send your scannable résumé, be certain the employer uses this technology. If you can't determine this, you may want to send two versions (scannable and traditional) to be sure your résumé gets considered.

Résumé Production and Other Tips

An ink-jet printer is the preferred option for printing your résumé. Begin by printing just a few copies. You may find a small error or you may simply want to make some changes, and it is less frustrating and less expensive if you print in small batches.

Résumé paper color should be carefully chosen. You should consider the types of employers who will receive your résumé and the types of positions for which you are applying. Use white or ivory paper for traditional or conservative employers or for higher-level positions.

Black ink on sharp, white paper can be harsh on the reader's eyes. Think about an ivory or cream paper that will provide less contrast and be easier to read. Pink, green, and blue tints should generally be avoided.

Many résumé writers buy packages of matching envelopes and cover sheet stationery that, although not absolutely necessary, help convey a professional impression.

If you'll be producing many cover letters at home, be sure you have high-quality printing equipment. Learn standard envelope formats for business, and retain a copy of every cover letter you send out. You can use the copies to take notes of any telephone conversations that may occur.

If attending a job fair, either carry a briefcase or place your résumé in a nicely covered legal-size pad holder.

The Cover Letter

The cover letter provides you with the opportunity to tailor your résumé by telling the prospective employer how you can be a benefit to the organization. It allows you to highlight aspects of your background that are not already discussed in your résumé and that might be especially relevant to the organization you are contacting or to the position you are seeking. Every résumé should have a cover letter enclosed when you send it out. Unlike the résumé, which may be mass-produced, a cover letter is most effective when it is individually prepared and focused on the particular requirements of the organization in question.

A good cover letter should supplement the résumé and motivate the reader to review the résumé. The format shown in Exhibit 2.3 is only a suggestion to help you decide what information to include in writing a cover letter.

Begin the cover letter with your street address six lines down from the top. Leave three to five lines between the date and the name of the person to whom you are addressing the cover letter. Make sure you leave one blank line between the salutation and the body of the letter and between paragraphs. After typing "Sincerely," leave four blank lines and type your name. This should leave plenty of room for your signature. A sample cover letter is shown in Exhibit 2.4.

The following guidelines will help you write good cover letters:

1. Be sure to type your letter neatly; ensure there are no misspellings.
2. Avoid unusual typefaces, such as script.
3. Address the letter to an individual, using the person's name and title. To obtain this information, call the company. If answering a blind newspaper advertisement, address the letter "To Whom It May Concern" or omit the salutation.
4. Be sure your cover letter directly indicates the position you are applying for and tells why you are qualified to fill it.
5. Send the original letter, not a photocopy, with your résumé. Keep a copy for your records.
6. Make your cover letter no more than one page.
7. Include a phone number where you can be reached.
8. Avoid trite language and have someone read the letter over to react to its tone, content, and mechanics.
9. For your own information, record the date you send out each letter and résumé.

Exhibit 2.3
COVER LETTER FORMAT

Your Street Address
Your Town, State, Zip
Phone Number
Fax Number
E-mail

Date

Name
Title
Organization
Address

Dear _____:

First Paragraph. In this paragraph state the reason for the letter, name the specific position or type of work you are applying for, and indicate from which resource (career services office, website, newspaper, contact, employment service) you learned of this opening. The first paragraph can also be used to inquire about future openings.

Second Paragraph. Indicate why you are interested in this position, the company, or its products or services, and what you can do for the employer. If you are a recent graduate, explain how your academic background makes you a qualified candidate. Try not to repeat the same information found in the résumé.

Third Paragraph. Refer the reader to the enclosed résumé for more detailed information.

Fourth Paragraph. In this paragraph say what you will do to follow up on your letter. For example, state that you will call by a certain date to set up an interview or to find out if the company will be recruiting in your area. Finish by indicating your willingness to answer any questions the recipient may have. Be sure you have provided your phone number.

Sincerely,

Type your name
Enclosure

Exhibit 2.4
SAMPLE COVER LETTER

13 Locust Street
San Diego, CA 98021
(619) 555-1111

October 12, 2002

Ken Kochien
Director of Development
Nature Conservancy Preserves
22 Main Street
Lockport, CA 98772

Dear Mr. Kochien:

In December of 2002, I will graduate from the San Diego campus of University College with a bachelor's degree in business management. I read of your opening for a capital campaign manager in *Community Jobs* (September 2002), and I am very interested in the possibilities it offers. I am writing to explore the opportunity for employment with the Nature Conservancy Preserves.

The advertisement indicated that you were looking for someone capable of coordinating meetings and producing campaign materials and donor acknowledgments. I believe my résumé outlines a work and education history that you will find interesting and relevant. Beginning with office duties and logistics for a renowned science conference for two summers early in high school, I gained some advertising and graphics experience with a local newspaper and my writing skills were polished working on our college weekly newspaper. Courses in psychology have added to my major course work and I have some excellent relevant experience working in our campus admissions office. I am productive, focused, and capable of producing high-quality work under time constraints.

As you will see by the enclosed résumé, I have had exposure to considerable technology here at college and am thoroughly familiar with all the software and database systems you mention in your ad. In addition, I have good spreadsheet experience and my word-processing skills are excellent.

continued

I would like to meet with you to discuss how my education and experience would be consistent with your needs. I will contact your office next week to discuss the possibility of an interview. In the meantime, if you have any questions or require additional information, please contact me at my home, (619) 555-1111.

Sincerely,

Mary Campbell
Enclosure

3

Researching Careers and Networking

Many business majors made their degree choice with the expectation that their degree would be the ticket to employment after graduation. But "business" is a vast field, populated with tens of thousands of job titles you have never heard of before. You know that a business major has given you an overview of management, marketing, accounting, economics, and organizational behavior. However, you still may be confused as to exactly what kinds of jobs you can do with your degree and what kinds of organizations will hire you. Are sales jobs reserved only for marketing majors? Where does a business major fit into a hospital or a museum, a department store chain or an environmental learning center?

What Do They Call the Job You Want?

One reason for confusion is perhaps a mistaken assumption that a college education provides job training. In most cases it does not. Of course, applied fields such as engineering, management, or education provide specific skills for the workplace as well as an education. Regardless, your overall college education exposes you to numerous fields of study and teaches you quantitative reasoning, critical thinking, writing, and speaking, all of which can be successfully applied to a number of different job fields. But it still remains up to you to choose a job field and to learn how to articulate the benefits of your education in a way the employer will appreciate.

Collecting Job Titles

The world of employment is a complex place, so you need to become a bit of an explorer and adventurer and be willing to try a variety of techniques to develop a list of possible occupations that might use your talents and education. You might find computerized interest inventories, reference books and other sources, and classified ads helpful in this respect. Once you have a list of possibilities that you are interested in and qualified for, you can move on to find out what kinds of organizations have these job titles.

Computerized Interest Inventories. One way to begin collecting job titles is to identify a number of jobs that call for your degree and the particular skills and interests you identified as part of the self-assessment process. There are excellent interactive career-guidance programs on the market to help you produce such selected lists of possible job titles. Most of these are available at colleges and at some larger town and city libraries. Two of the industry leaders are *CHOICES* and *DISCOVER*. Both allow you to enter interests, values, educational background, and other information to produce lists of possible occupations and industries. Each of the resources listed here will produce different job title lists. Some job titles will appear again and again, while others will be unique to a particular source. Investigate all of them!

Reference Sources. Books on the market that may be available through your local library or career counseling office also suggest various occupations related to specific majors. The following are only a few of the many good books on the market: *The College Board Guide to 150 Popular College Majors, College Majors and Careers: A Resource Guide for Effective Life Planning* both by Paul Phifer, and *Kaplan's What to Study: 101 Fields in a Flash.* All of these books list possible job titles within the academic major.

For business majors, approximately eighty-two job titles are listed. Some are familiar ones, such as sales agent or retail manager, hospital administrator, and financial analyst. Others are interestingly different, such as import-export agent, job analyst, or conciliator.

The *Occupational Thesaurus* is another good resource, which lists job title possibilities under general categories. So, if as a business major you discovered retail manager as a job title in the book *What Can I Do with a Major in . . . ?*, you can then go to the *Occupational Thesaurus*, which lists scores of jobs under that title. Under "Merchandising" there is a list of over forty associated job titles, including inventory control, operations management, economic forecasting, customer relations, and new business research. If retail management was a suggested job title for you, this source adds some depth by suggesting a number of different occupational settings.

Each job title deserves your consideration. Like removing the layers of an onion, the search for job titles can go on and on! As you spend time doing this activity, you are actually learning more about the value of your degree. What's important in your search at this point is not to become critical or selective but rather to develop as long a list of possibilities as you can. Every source used will help you add new and potentially exciting jobs to your growing list.

Classified Ads. It has been well publicized that the classified ad section of the newspaper represents only a small fraction of the current job market. Nevertheless, the weekly classified ads can be a great help to you in your search. Although they may not be the best place to look for a job, they can teach you a lot about the job market. Classified ads provide a good education in job descriptions, duties, responsibilities, and qualifications. In addition, they provide insight into which industries are actively recruiting and some indication of the area's employment market. This is particularly helpful when seeking a position in a specific geographic area and/or a specific field. For your purposes, classified ads are a good source for job titles to add to your list.

Read the Sunday classified ads in a major market newspaper for several weeks in a row. Cut and paste all the ads that interest you and seem to call for something close to your education, skills, experience, and interests. Remember that classified ads are written for what an organization *hopes* to find, you don't have to meet absolutely every criterion. However, if certain requirements are stated as absolute minimums and you cannot meet them, it's best not to waste your time and that of the employer.

The weekly classified want ads exercise is important because these jobs are out in the marketplace. They truly exist, and people with your qualifications are being sought to apply. What's more, many of these advertisements describe the duties and responsibilities of the job advertised and give you a beginning sense of the challenges and opportunities such a position presents. Some will indicate salary, and that will be helpful as well. This information will better define the jobs for you and provide some good material for possible interviews in that field.

Exploring Job Descriptions

Once you've arrived at a solid list of possible job titles that interest you and for which you believe you are somewhat qualified, it's a good idea to do some research on each of these jobs. The preeminent source for such job information is the *Dictionary of Occupational Titles*, or *DOT* (wave.net/upg/immigration/dot_index.html). This directory lists every conceivable job and provides excellent up-to-date information on duties and responsibilities, interactions with associates, and day-to-day assignments and tasks. These descriptions provide a thorough job analysis, but they do not consider the possible employers or the environments in which a job may be performed. So, although a position as public relations officer may be well defined in terms of duties and responsibilities, it does not explain the differences in doing public relations work in a college or a hospital or a factory or a bank. You will need to look somewhere else for work settings.

Learning More About Possible Work Settings

After reading some job descriptions, you may choose to edit and revise your list of job titles once again, discarding those you feel are not suitable and keeping those that continue to hold your interest. Or you may wish to keep your list intact and see where these jobs may be located. For example, if you are interested in public relations and you appear to have those skills and the requisite education, you'll want to know what organizations do public relations. How can you find that out? How much income does someone in public relations make a year and what is the employment potential for the field of public relations?

To answer these and many other questions about your list of job titles, we recommend you try any of the following resources: *Careers Encyclopedia*, the professional societies and resources found throughout this book, *College to Career: The Guide to Job Opportunities*, and the *Occupational Outlook Handbook* (http://stats.bls.gov/ocohome.htm). Each of these resources, in a different way, will help to put the job titles you have selected into an employer context. Perhaps the most extensive discussion is found in the *Occupational Outlook Handbook*, which gives a thorough presentation of the nature of the work, the working conditions, employment statistics, training, other qualifications, and advancement possibilities as well as job outlook and earnings. Related occupations are also detailed, and a select bibliography is provided to help you find additional information.

Continuing with our public relations example, your search through these reference materials would teach you that the public relations jobs you find attractive are available in larger hospitals, financial institutions, most corporations (both consumer goods and industrial goods), media organizations, and colleges and universities.

Networking

Networking is the process of deliberately establishing relationships to get career-related information or to alert potential employers that you are available for work. Networking is critically important to today's job seeker for two reasons: it will help you get the information you need, and it can help you find out about *all* of the available jobs.

Getting the Information You Need

Networkers will review your résumé and give you feedback on its effectiveness. They will talk about the job you are looking for and give you a candid appraisal of how they see your strengths and weaknesses. If they have a good sense of the industry or the employment sector for that job, you'll get their feelings on future trends in the industry as well. Some networkers will be very forthcoming about salaries, job-hunting techniques, and suggestions for your job search strategy. Many have been known to place calls right from the interview desk to friends and associates who might be interested in you. Each networker will make his or her own contribution, and each will be valuable.

Because organizations must evolve to adapt to current global market needs, the information provided by decision makers within various organizations will be critical to your success as a new job market entrant. For example, you might learn about the concept of virtual organizations from a networker. Virtual organizations coordinate economic activity to deliver value to customers by using resources outside the traditional boundaries of the organization. This concept is being discussed and implemented by chief executive officers of many organizations, including Ford Motor, Dell, and IBM. Networking can help you find out about this and other trends currently affecting the industries under your consideration.

Finding Out About All of the Available Jobs

Not every job that is available at this very moment is advertised for potential applicants to see. This is called the *hidden job market*. Only 15 to 20 percent of all jobs are formally advertised, which means that 80 to 85 percent of available jobs do not appear in published channels. Networking will help you become more knowledgeable about all the employment opportunities available during your job search period.

Although someone you might talk to today doesn't know of any openings within his or her organization, tomorrow or next week or next month an opening may occur. If you've taken the time to show an interest in and knowledge of their organization, if you've shown the company representative how you can help achieve organizational goals and that you can fit into the organization, you'll be one of the first candidates considered for the position.

Networking: A Proactive Approach

Networking is a proactive rather than a reactive approach. You, as a job seeker, are expected to initiate a certain level of activity on your own behalf; you cannot afford to simply respond to jobs listed in the newspaper. Being proactive means building a network of contacts that includes informed and interested decision makers who will provide you with up-to-date knowledge of the current job market and increase your chances of finding out about employment opportunities appropriate for your interests, experience, and level of education. An old axiom of networking says, "You are only two phone calls away from the information you need." In other words, by talking to enough people, you will quickly come across someone who can offer you help.

Preparing to Network

In deliberately establishing relationships, maximize your efforts by organizing your approach. Five specific areas in which you can organize your efforts include reviewing your self-assessment, reviewing your research on job sites and organizations, deciding who it is you want to talk to, keeping track of all your efforts, and creating your self-promotion tools.

Review Your Self-Assessment

Your self-assessment is as important a tool in preparing to network as it has been in other aspects of your job search. You have carefully evaluated your personal traits, personal values, economic needs, longer-term goals, skill base, preferred skills, and underdeveloped skills. During the networking process you will be called upon to communicate what you know about yourself and relate it to the information or job you seek. Be sure to review the exercises that you completed in the self-assessment section of this book in preparation for networking. We've explained that you need to assess what skills you have acquired from your major that are of general value to an employer and to be ready to express those in ways employers can appreciate as useful in their own organizations.

Review Research on Job Sites and Organizations

In addition, individuals assisting you will expect that you'll have at least some background information on the occupation or industry of interest to you. Refer to the appropriate sections of this book and other relevant publications to acquire the background information necessary for effective networking. They'll explain how to identify not only the job titles that might be of interest to you but also what kinds of organizations employ people to do that job. You will develop some sense of working conditions and expectations about duties and responsibilities—all of which will be of help in your networking interviews.

Decide Who It Is You Want to Talk To

Networking cannot begin until you decide who it is that you want to talk to and, in general, what type of information you hope to gain from your contacts. Once you know this, it's time to begin developing a list of contacts. Five useful sources for locating contacts are described here.

College Alumni Network. Most colleges and universities have created a formal network of alumni and friends of the institution who are particularly interested in helping currently enrolled students and graduates of their alma mater gain employment-related information.

Because the business major covers such a broad spectrum of human activity, you'll find business majors employed in every sector of the economy: government, business, and nonprofit. The diversity of employment as evidenced by an alumni list from your college or university should be encouraging and informative to the business graduate. Among such a diversified group, there are likely to be scores you would enjoy talking with and perhaps could meet. Some might be working quite far from you, but that does not preclude a telephone call or exchange of correspondence.

It is usually a simple process to make use of an alumni network. Visit your college's website and locate the alumni office and/or your career center. Either or both sites will have information about your school's alumni network. You'll be provided with information on shadowing experiences, geographic information, or those alumni offering job referrals. If you don't find what you're looking for, don't hesitate to phone or E-mail your career center and ask what they can do to help you connect with an alum.

Alumni networkers may provide some combination of the following services: day-long shadowing experiences, telephone interviews, in-person interviews, information on relocating to given geographic areas, internship information, suggestions on graduate school study, and job vacancy notices.

> What a valuable experience! If you are interested in a nonprofit administrative position, you may be concerned about your degree preparation and whether you would be considered eligible to work in this field. Spending a day with an alumnus who works as an administrator for a nonprofit, asking questions about his or her educational preparation and training, will give you a more concrete view of the possibilities for your degree. Observing firsthand how this person does the job and exactly what the job entails provides far better decision criteria for you than just reading on the subject could possibly provide.

Present and Former Supervisors. If you believe you are on good terms with present or former job supervisors, they may be an excellent resource for providing information or directing you to appropriate resources that would have information related to your current interests and needs. Additionally, these supervisors probably belong to professional organizations that they might be willing to utilize to get information for you.

> If, for example, you were interested in working as a buyer or merchandise manager for a major department store, and you are currently working on the wait staff of a local restaurant, talk with your supervisor or the owner. He or she may belong to the local Chamber of Commerce, whose director might have information on members affiliated with retail stores in your area. You would

probably be able to obtain the names and business telephone numbers of those people, which would allow you to begin the networking process.

Employers in Your Area. Although you may be interested in working in a geographic location different from the one where you currently reside, don't overlook the value of the knowledge and contacts those around you are able to provide. Use the local telephone directory and newspaper to identify the types of organizations you are thinking of working for or professionals who have the kinds of jobs you are interested in. Recently, a call made to a local hospital's financial administrator for information on working in health-care financial administration yielded more pertinent information on training seminars, regional professional organizations, and potential employment sites than a national organization was willing to provide.

Employers in Geographic Areas Where You Hope to Work. If you are thinking about relocating, identifying prospective employers or informational contacts in the new location will be critical to your success. Here are some tips for online searching. First, use a "metasearch" engine to get the most out of your search. Metasearch engines combine several engines into one powerful tool. We frequently use dogpile.com and metasearch.com for this purpose. Try using the city and state as your keywords in a search. *New Haven, Connecticut* will bring you to the city's website with links to the chamber of commerce, member businesses, and other valuable resources. By using looksmart.com you can locate newspapers in any area, and they, too, can provide valuable insight before you relocate. Of course, both dogpile and metasearch can lead you to yellow and white page directories in areas you are considering.

Professional Associations and Organizations. Professional associations and organizations can provide valuable information in several areas: career paths that you might not have considered, qualifications relating to those career choices, publications that list current job openings, and workshops or seminars that will enhance your professional knowledge and skills. They can also be excellent sources for background information on given industries: their health, current problems, and future challenges.

There are several excellent resources available to help you locate professional associations and organizations that would have information to meet your needs. Two especially useful publications are the *Encyclopedia of Associations* and *National Trade and Professional Associations of the United States.*

Keep Track of All Your Efforts

It can be difficult, almost impossible, to remember all the details related to each contact you make during the networking process, so you will want to develop a record-keeping system that works for you. Formalize this process by using your computer to keep a record of the people and organizations you want to contact. You can simply record the contact's name, address, and telephone number, and what information you hope to gain.

You could record this as a simple Word document and you could still use the "Find" function if you were trying to locate some data and could only recall the firm's name or the contact's name. If you're comfortable with database management and you have some database software on your computer, then you can put information at your fingertips even if you have only the zip code! The point here is not technological sophistication but good record keeping.

Once you have created this initial list, it will be helpful to keep more detailed information as you begin to actually make the contacts. Those details should include complete contact information, the date and content of each contact, names and information for additional networkers, and required follow-up. Don't forget to send a letter thanking your contact for his or her time! Your contact will appreciate your recall of details of your meetings and conversations, and the information will help you to focus your networking efforts.

Create Your Self-Promotion Tools

There are two types of promotional tools that are used in the networking process. The first is a résumé and cover letter, and the second is a one-minute "infomercial," which may be given over the telephone or in person.

Techniques for writing an effective résumé and cover letter are discussed in Chapter 2. Once you have reviewed that material and prepared these important documents, you will have created one of your self-promotion tools.

The one-minute infomercial will demand that you begin tying your interests, abilities, and skills to the people or organizations you want to network with. Think about your goal for making the contact to help you understand what you should say about yourself. You should be able to express yourself easily and convincingly. If, for example, you are contacting an alumnus of your institution to obtain the names of possible employment sites in a distant city, be prepared to discuss why you are interested in moving to that location, the types of jobs you are interested in, and the skills and abilities you possess that will make you a qualified candidate.

To create a meaningful one-minute infomercial, write it out, practice it as if it will be a spoken presentation, rewrite it, and practice it again if necessary until expressing yourself comes easily and is convincing.

Here's a simplified example of an infomercial for use over the telephone:

Hello, Mr. Billow? My name is Mindy Howard. I am a recent graduate of West Coast College, and I wish to enter the health-care field. I feel confident I have many of the skills I understand are valued for administrators in health care. I have a strong quantitative background, with good research and computer skills. In addition, I have excellent interpersonal skills and am known as a compassionate, caring individual. I understand these are valuable traits in your line of work!

Mr. Billow, I'm calling you because I still need more information about the health-care field and where I might fit in. I'm hoping you'll have time to sit down with me for about half an hour and discuss your perspective on careers in health-care administration with me. There are so many possible employers to approach, and I am seeking some advice on which might be the best bet for my particular combination of skills and experience.

Would you be willing to do that for me? I would greatly appreciate it. I am available most mornings, if that's convenient for you.

It very well may happen that your employer contact wishes you to communicate by E-mail. The infomercial quoted above could easily be rewritten for an E-mail message. You should "cut and paste" your résumé right into the E-mail text itself.

Other effective self-promotion tools include portfolios for those in the arts, writing professions, or teaching. Portfolios show examples of work, photographs of projects or classroom activities, or certificates and credentials that are job related. There may not be an opportunity to use the portfolio during an interview, and it is not something that should be left with the organization. It is designed to be explained and displayed by the creator. However, during some networking meetings, there may be an opportunity to illustrate a point or strengthen a qualification by exhibiting the portfolio.

Beginning the Networking Process

Set the Tone for Your Communications

It can be useful to establish "tone words" for any communications you embark upon. Before making your first telephone call or writing your first letter, decide what you want the person to think of you. If you are networking to try to obtain a job, your tone words might include descriptors such as *genuine*, *informed*, and *self-knowledgeable*. When you're trying to acquire information, your tone words may have a slightly different focus, such as *courteous*, *organized*, *focused*, and *well-spoken*. Use the tone words you establish for your contacts to guide you through the networking process.

Honestly Express Your Intentions

When contacting individuals, it is important to be honest about your reasons for making the contact. Establish your purpose in your own mind and be able and ready to articulate it concisely. Determine an initial agenda, whether it be informational questioning or self-promotion, present it to your contact, and be ready to respond immediately. If you don't adequately prepare before initiating your overture, you may find yourself at a disadvantage if you're asked to immediately begin your informational interview or self-promotion during the first phone conversation or visit.

Start Networking Within Your Circle of Confidence

Once you have organized your approach—by utilizing specific researching methods, creating a system for keeping track of the people you will contact, and developing effective self-promotion tools—you are ready to begin networking. The best way to begin networking is by talking with a group of people you trust and feel comfortable with. This group is usually made up of your family, friends, and career counselors. No matter who is in this inner circle, they will have a special interest in seeing you succeed in your job search. In addition, because they will be easy to talk to, you should try taking some risks in terms of practicing your information-seeking approach. Gain confidence in talking about the strengths you bring to an organization and the underdeveloped skills you feel hinder your candidacy. Be sure to review the section on self-assessment for tips on approaching each of these areas.

Ask for critical but constructive feedback from the people in your circle of confidence on the letters you write and the one-minute infomercial you have developed. Evaluate whether you want to make the changes they suggest, then practice the changes on others within this circle.

Stretch the Boundaries of Your Networking Circle of Confidence

Once you have refined the promotional tools you will use to accomplish your networking goals, you will want to make additional contacts. Because you will not know most of these people, it will be a less comfortable activity to undertake. The practice that you gained with your inner circle of trusted friends should have prepared you to now move outside of that comfort zone.

It is said that any information a person needs is only two phone calls away, but the information cannot be gained until you (1) make a reasonable guess about who might have the information you need and (2) pick up the telephone to make the call. Using your network list that includes alumni, instructors, supervisors, employers, and associations, you can begin preparing your list of questions that will allow you to get the information you need.

Prepare the Questions You Want to Ask

Networkers can provide you with the insider's perspective on any given field and you can ask them questions that you might not want to ask in an interview. For example, you can ask them to describe the more repetitious or mundane parts of the job or ask them for a realistic idea of salary expectations. Be sure to prepare your questions ahead of time so that you are organized and efficient.

Be Prepared to Answer Some Questions

To communicate effectively, you must anticipate questions that will be asked of you by the networkers you contact. Revisit the self-assessment process you undertook and the research you've done so that you can effortlessly respond to questions about your short- and long-term goals and the kinds of jobs you are most interested in pursuing.

General Networking Tips

Make Every Contact Count. Setting the tone for each interaction is critical. Approaches that will help you communicate in an effective way include politeness, being appreciative of time provided to you, and being prepared and thorough. Remember, *everyone* within an organization has a circle of influence, so be prepared to interact effectively with each person you encounter in the networking process, including secretarial and support staff. Many information or job seekers have thwarted their own efforts by being rude to some individuals they encountered as they networked because they made the incorrect assumption that certain persons were unimportant.

Sometimes your contacts may be surprised at their ability to help you. After meeting and talking with you, they might think they have not offered much in the way of help. A day or two later, however, they may make a contact that would be useful to you and refer you to that person.

With Each Contact, Widen Your Circle of Networkers. Always leave an informational interview with the names of at least two more people who can help you get the information or job that you are seeking. Don't be shy about asking for additional contacts; networking is all about increasing the number of people you can interact with to achieve your goals.

Make Your Own Decisions. As you talk with different people and get answers to the questions you pose, you may hear conflicting information or get conflicting suggestions. Your job is to listen to these "experts" and decide what information and which suggestions will help you achieve *your* goals. Only implement those suggestions that you believe will work for you.

Shutting Down Your Network

As you achieve the goals that motivated your networking activity—getting the information you need or the job you want—the time will come to inactivate all or parts of your network. As you do, be sure to tell your primary supporters about your change in status. Call or write to each one of them and give them as many details about your new status as you feel is necessary to maintain a positive relationship.

Because a network takes on a life of its own, activity undertaken on your behalf will continue even after you cease your efforts. As you get calls or are contacted in some fashion, be sure to inform these networkers about your change in status, and thank them for assistance they have provided.

Information on the latest employment trends indicates that workers will change jobs or careers several times in their lifetime. Networking, then, will be a critical aspect in the span of your professional life. If you carefully and thoughtfully conduct your networking activities during your job search, you will have a solid foundation of experience when you need to network the next time around.

Where Are These Jobs, Anyway?

Having a list of job titles that you've designed around your own career interests and skills is an excellent beginning. It means you've really thought about who you are and what you are presenting to the employment market. It has caused you to think seriously about the most appealing environments to work in, and you have identified some employer types that represent these environments.

The research and the thinking that you've done thus far will be used again and again. They will be helpful in writing your résumé and cover letters, in talking about yourself on the telephone to prospective employers, and in answering interview questions.

Now is a good time to begin to narrow the field of job titles and employment sites down to some specific employers to initiate the employment contact.

Finding Out Which Employers Hire People Like You

This section will provide tips, techniques, and specific resources for developing an actual list of specific employers that can be used to make contacts. It is only an outline that you must be prepared to tailor to your own particular needs and according to what you bring to the job search. Once again, it is important to communicate with others along the way exactly what you're looking for and what your goals are for the research you're doing. Librarians, employers, career counselors, friends, friends of friends, business contacts, and bookstore staff will all have helpful information on geographically specific and new resources to aid you in locating employers who'll hire you.

Identifying Information Resources

Your interview wardrobe and your new résumé might have put a dent in your wallet, but the resources you'll need to pursue your job search are available for free. The categories of information detailed here are not hard to find and are yours for the browsing.

Numerous resources described in this section will help you identify actual employers. Use all of them or any others that you identify as available in your geographic area. As you become experienced in this process, you'll quickly figure out which information sources are helpful and which are not. If you live in a rural area, a well-planned day trip to a major city that includes a college career office, a large college or city library, state and federal employment centers, a chamber of commerce office, and a well-stocked bookstore can produce valuable results.

There are many excellent resources available to help you identify actual job sites. They are categorized into employer directories (usually indexed by product lines and geographic location), geographically based directories (designed to highlight particular cities, regions, or states), career-specific directories (e.g., *Sports MarketPlace*, which lists tens of thousands of firms involved with sports), periodicals and newspapers, targeted job posting publications, and videos. This is by no means meant to be a complete treatment of resources but rather a starting point for identifying useful resources.

Working from the more general references to highly specific resources, we provide a basic list to help you begin your search. Many of these you'll find easily available. In some cases reference librarians and others will suggest even better materials for your particular situation. Start to create your own customized bibliography of job search references.

Geographically Based Directories. The Job Bank series published by Bob Adams, Inc. (aip.com) contains detailed entries on each area's major employers, including business activity, address, phone number, and hiring contact name. Many listings specify educational backgrounds being sought in potential employees. Each volume contains a solid discussion of each city's or state's major employment sectors. Organizations are also indexed by industry. Job Bank volumes are available for the following places: Atlanta, Boston, Chicago, Dallas–Ft. Worth, Denver, Detroit, Florida, Houston, Los Angeles, Minneapolis, New York, Ohio, Philadelphia, San Francisco, Seattle, St. Louis, Washington, D.C., and other cities throughout the Northwest.

National Job Bank (careercity.com) lists employers in every state, along with contact names and commonly hired job categories. Included are many small companies often overlooked by other directories. Companies are also indexed by industry. This publication provides information on educational backgrounds sought and lists company benefits.

Periodicals and Newspapers. Several sources are available to help you locate which journals or magazines carry job advertisements in your field. Other resources help you identify opportunities in other parts of the country.

- *Where the Jobs Are: A Comprehensive Directory of 1200 Journals Listing Career Opportunities*
- *Corptech Fast 5000 Company Locator*
- *National Ad Search* (nationaladsearch.com)
- *The Federal Jobs Digest* (jobsfed.com) and *Federal Career Opportunities*
- *World Chamber of Commerce Directory* (chamberofcommerce.org)

This list is certainly not exhaustive; use it to begin your job search work.

Targeted Job Posting Publications. Although the resources that follow are national in scope, they are either targeted to one medium of contact (telephone), focused on specific types of jobs, or less comprehensive than the sources previously listed.

- Job Hotlines USA (careers.org/topic/01_002.html)
- *The Job Hunter* (jobhunter.com)
- *Current Jobs for Graduates* (graduatejobs.com)
- *Environmental Opportunities* (ecojobs.com)
- *Y National Vacancy List* (ymcahrm.ns.ca/employed/jobleads.html)
- *ARTSearch*
- *Community Jobs*
- *National Association of Colleges and Employers: Job Choices series*
- *National Association of Colleges and Employers* (naceweb.org)

Videos. You may be one of the many job seekers who likes to get information via a medium other than paper. Many career libraries, public libraries, and career centers in libraries carry an assortment of videos that will help you learn new techniques and get information helpful in the job search.

Locating Information Resources

Throughout these introductory chapters, we have continually referred you to various websites for information on everything from job listings to career information. Using the Web gives you a mobility at your computer that you don't enjoy if you rely solely on books or newspapers or printed journals. Moreover, material on the Web, if the site is maintained, can be the most up-to-date information available.

You'll eventually identify the information resources that work best for you, but make certain you've covered the full range of resources before you begin to rely on a smaller list. Here's a short list of informational sites that many job seekers find helpful:

- Public and college libraries
- College career centers
- Bookstores
- The Internet
- Local and state government personnel offices
- Career/job fairs

Each one of these sites offers a collection of resources that will help you get the information you need.

As you meet and talk with service professionals at all these sites, be sure to let them know what you're doing. Inform them of your job search, what you've already accomplished, and what you're looking for. The more people who know you're job seeking, the greater the possibility that someone will have information or know someone who can help you along your way.

4

Interviewing and Job Offer Considerations

Certainly, there can be no one part of the job search process more fraught with anxiety and worry than the interview. Yet seasoned job seekers welcome the interview and will often say, "Just get me an interview and I'm on my way!" They understand that the interview is crucial to the hiring process and equally crucial for them, as job candidates, to have the opportunity of a personal dialogue to add to what the employer may already have learned from the résumé, cover letter, and telephone conversations.

Believe it or not, the interview is to be welcomed, and even enjoyed! It is a perfect opportunity for you, the candidate, to sit down with an employer and express yourself and display who you are and what you want. Of course, it takes thought and planning and a little strategy; after all, it *is* a job interview! But it can be a positive, if not pleasant, experience and one you can look back on and feel confident about your performance and effort.

For many new job seekers, a job, any job, seems a wonderful thing. But seasoned interview veterans know that the job interview is an important step for both sides—the employer and the candidate—to see what each has to offer and whether there is going to be a "fit" of personalities, work styles, and attitudes. And it is this concept of balance in the interview, that both sides have important parts to play, that holds the key to success in mastering this aspect of the job search strategy.

Try to think of the interview as a conversation between two interested and equal partners. You both have important, even vital, information to deliver and to learn. Of course, there's no denying the employer has some leverage, especially in the initial interview for recruitment or any interview scheduled by the candidate and not the recruiter. That should not prevent the interviewee from seeking to play an equal part in what should be a fair exchange of information. Too often the untutored candidate allows the interview to become one-sided. The employer asks all the questions and the candidate simply responds. The ideal would be for two mutually interested parties to sit down and discuss possibilities for each. This is a conversation of significance, and it requires preparation, thought about the tone of the interview, and planning of the nature and details of the information to be exchanged.

Preparing for the Interview

The length of most initial interviews is about thirty minutes. Given the brevity, the information that is exchanged ought to be important. The candidate should be delivering material that the employer cannot discover on the résumé, and in turn, the candidate should be learning things about the employer that he or she could not otherwise find out. After all, if you have only thirty minutes, why waste time on information that is already published? The information exchanged is more than just factual, and both sides will learn much from what they see of each other, as well. How the candidate looks, speaks, and acts are important to the employer. The employer's attention to the interview and awareness of the candidate's résumé, the setting, and the quality of information presented are important to the candidate.

Just as the employer has every right to be disappointed when a prospect is late for the interview, looks unkempt, and seems ill-prepared to answer fairly standard questions, the candidate may be disappointed with an interviewer who isn't ready for the meeting, hasn't learned the basic résumé facts, and is constantly interrupted by telephone calls. In either situation there's good reason to feel let down.

There are many elements to a successful interview, and some of them are not easy to describe or prepare for. Sometimes there is just a chemistry between interviewer and interviewee that brings out the best in both, and a good exchange takes place. But there is much the candidate can do to pave the way for success in terms of his or her résumé, personal appearance, goals, and interview strategy—each of which we will discuss. However, none of this preparation is as important as the time and thought the candidate gives to personal self-assessment.

Self-Assessment
Neither a stunning résumé nor an expensive, well-tailored suit can compensate for candidates who do not know what they want, where they are going,

or why they are interviewing with a particular employer. Self-assessment, the process by which we begin to know and acknowledge our own particular blend of education, experiences, needs, and goals, is not something that can be sorted out the weekend before a major interview. Of all the elements of interview preparation, this one requires the longest lead time and cannot be faked.

Because the time allotted for most interviews is brief, it is all the more important for job candidates to understand and express succinctly why they are there and what they have to offer. This is not a time for undue modesty (or for braggadocio either); it is a time for a compelling, reasoned statement of why you feel that you and this employer might make a good match. It means you have to have thought about your skills, interests, and attributes; related those to your life experiences and your own history of challenges and opportunities; and determined what that indicates about your strengths, preferences, values, and areas needing further development.

If you need some assistance with self-assessment issues, refer to Chapter 1. Included are suggested exercises that can be done as needed, such as making up an experiential diary and extracting obvious strengths and weaknesses from past experiences. These simple assignments will help you look at past activities as collections of tasks with accompanying skills and responsibilities. Don't overlook your high school or college career office. Many offer personal counseling on self-assessment issues and may provide testing instruments such as the *Myers-Briggs Type Indicator (MBTI)*, the *Harrington-O'Shea Career Decision-Making System (CDM)*, the *Strong Interest Inventory (SII)*, or any other of a wide selection of assessment tools that can help you clarify some of these issues prior to the interview stage of your job search.

The Résumé

Résumé preparation has been discussed in detail, and some basic examples were provided. In this section we want to concentrate on how best to use your résumé in the interview. In most cases the employer will have seen the résumé prior to the interview, and, in fact, it may well have been the quality of that résumé that secured the interview opportunity.

An interview is a conversation, however, and not an exercise in reading. So, if the employer hasn't seen your résumé and you have brought it along to the interview, wait until asked or until the end of the interview to offer it. Otherwise, you may find yourself staring at the back of your résumé and simply answering "yes" and "no" to a series of questions drawn from that document.

Sometimes an interviewer is not prepared and does not know or recall the contents of the résumé and may use the résumé to a greater or lesser degree as a "prompt" during the interview. It is for you to judge what that may indicate about the individual performing the interview or the employer. If your interviewer seems surprised by the scheduled meeting, relies on the résumé to an inordinate degree, and seems otherwise unfamiliar with your background, this lack of preparation for the hiring process could well be a symptom of general management disorganization or may simply be the result of poor planning on the part of one individual. It is your responsibility as a potential employee to be aware of these signals and make your decisions accordingly.

In any event, it is perfectly acceptable for you to get the conversation back to a more interpersonal style by saying something like, "Mr. Smith, you might be interested in some recent experience I gained in a volunteer position at our local hospital that is not detailed on my résumé. May I tell you about it?" This can return the interview to two people talking to each other, not one reading and the other responding.

By all means, bring at least one copy of your résumé to the interview. Occasionally, at the close of an interview, an interviewer will express an interest in circulating a résumé to several departments, and you could then offer the copy you brought. Sometimes, an interview appointment provides an opportunity to meet others in the organization who may express an interest in you and your background, and it may be helpful to follow up with a copy of your résumé. Our best advice, however, is to keep it out of sight until needed or requested.

Employer Information

Whether your interview is for graduate school admission, an overseas corporate position, or a position with a local company, it is important to know something about the employer or the organization. Keeping in mind that the interview is relatively brief and that you will hopefully have other interviews with other organizations, it is important to keep your research in proportion. If secondary interviews are called for, you will have additional time to do further research. For the first interview, it is helpful to know the organization's mission, goals, size, scope of operations, and so forth. Your research may uncover recent areas of challenge or particular successes that may help to fuel the interview. Use the "What Do They Call the Job You Want?" section of Chapter 3, your library, and your career or guidance office to help you locate this information in the most efficient way possible. Don't be shy in asking advice of these counseling and guidance professionals on how best to spend your preparation time. With some practice, you'll soon learn how much information is enough and which kinds of information are most useful to you.

Interview Content

We've already discussed how it can help to think of the interview as an important conversation—one that, as with any conversation, you want to find pleasant and interesting and to leave you with a good feeling. But because this conversation is especially important, the information that's exchanged is critical to its success. What do you want them to know about you? What do you need to know about them? What interview technique do you need to particularly pay attention to? How do you want to manage the close of the interview? What steps will follow in the hiring process?

Except for the professional interviewer, most of us find interviewing stressful and anxiety-provoking. Developing a strategy before you begin interviewing will help you relieve some stress and anxiety. One particular strategy that has worked for many and may work for you is interviewing by objective. Before you interview, write down three to five goals you would like to achieve for that interview. They may be technique goals: smile a little more, have a firmer handshake, be sure to ask about the next stage in the interview process before leaving. They may be content-oriented goals: find out about the company's current challenges and opportunities; be sure to speak of your recent research, writing experiences, or foreign travel. Whatever your goals, jot down a few of them as goals for each interview.

Most people find that in trying to achieve these few goals, their interviewing technique becomes more organized and focused. After the interview, the most common question friends and family ask is "How did it go?" With this technique, you have an indication of whether you met *your* goals for the meeting, not just some vague idea of how it went. Chances are, if you accomplished what you wanted to, it improved the quality of the entire interview. As you continue to interview, you will want to revise your goals to continue improving your interview skills.

Now, add to the concept of the significant conversation the idea of a beginning, a middle, and a closing and you will have two thoughts that will give your interview a distinctive character. Be sure to make your introduction warm and cordial. Say your full name (and if it's a difficult-to-pronounce name, help the interviewer to pronounce it) and make certain you know your interviewer's name and how to pronounce it. Most interviews begin with some "soft talk" about the weather, chat about the candidate's trip to the interview site, or national events. This is done as a courtesy to relax both you and the interviewer, to get you talking, and to generally try to defuse the atmosphere of excessive tension. Try to be yourself, engage in the conversation, and don't try to second-guess the interviewer. This is simply what it appears to be—casual conversation.

Once you and the interviewer move on to exchange more serious information in the middle part of the interview, the two most important concerns become your ability to handle challenging questions and your success at asking meaningful ones. Interviewer questions will probably fall into one of three categories: personal assessment and career direction, academic assessment, and knowledge of the employer. Here are a few examples of questions in each category:

Personal Assessment and Career Direction
1. What motivates you to put forth your best effort?
2. What do you consider to be your greatest strengths and weaknesses?
3. What qualifications do you have that make you think you will be successful in this career?

Academic Assessment
1. What led you to choose your major?
2. What subjects did you like best and least? Why?
3. How has your college experience prepared you for this career?

Knowledge of the Employer
1. What do you think it takes to be successful in an organization like ours?
2. In what ways do you think you can make a contribution to our organization?
3. Why did you choose to seek a position with this organization?

The interviewer wants a response to each question but is also gauging your enthusiasm, preparedness, and willingness to communicate. In each response you should provide some information about yourself that can be related to the employer's needs. A common mistake is to give too much information. Answer each question completely, but be careful not to run on too long with extensive details or examples.

Questions About Underdeveloped Skills

Most employers interview people who have met some minimum criteria of education and experience. They interview candidates to see who they are, to learn what kind of personality they exhibit, and to get some sense of how this person might fit into the existing organization. It may be that you are asked about skills the employer hopes to find and that you have not documented. Maybe it's grant-writing experience, knowledge of the European political system, or a knowledge of the film world.

To questions about skills and experiences you don't have, answer honestly and forthrightly and try to offer some additional information about skills you do have. For example, perhaps the employer is disappointed you have no grant-writing experience. An honest answer may be as follows:

No, unfortunately, I was never in a position to acquire those skills. I do understand something of the complexities of the grant-writing process and feel confident that my attention to detail, careful reading skills, and strong writing would make grants a wonderful challenge in a new job. I think I could get up on the learning curve quickly.

The employer hears an honest admission of lack of experience but is reassured by some specific skill details that do relate to grant writing and a confident manner that suggests enthusiasm and interest in a challenge.

For many students, questions about their possible contribution to an employer's organization can prove challenging. Because your education has probably not included specific training for a job, you need to review your academic record and select capabilities you have developed in your major that an employer can appreciate. For example, perhaps you read well and can analyze and condense what you've read into smaller, more focused pieces. That could be valuable. Or maybe you did some serious research and you know you have valuable investigative skills. Your public speaking might be highly developed and you might use visual aids appropriately and effectively. Or maybe your skill at correspondence, memos, and messages is effective. Whatever it is, you must take it out of the academic context and put it into a new, employer-friendly context so your interviewer can best judge how you could help the organization.

Exhibiting knowledge of the organization will, without a doubt, show the interviewer that you are interested enough in the available position to have done some legwork in preparation for the interview. Remember, it is not necessary to know every detail of the organization's history but rather to have a general knowledge about why it is in business and how the industry is faring.

Sometime during the interview, generally after the midway point, you'll be asked if you have any questions for the interviewer. Your questions will tell the employer much about your attitude and your desire to understand the organization's expectations so you can compare them to your own strengths. The following are just a few questions you might want to ask:

1. What is the communication style of the organization? (meetings, memos, and so forth)
2. What would a typical day in this position be like for me?
3. What have been some of the interesting challenges and opportunities your organization has recently faced?

Most interviews draw to a natural closing point, so be careful not to prolong the discussion. At a signal from the interviewer, wind up your presentation, express your appreciation for the opportunity, and be sure to ask what the next stage in the process will be. When can you expect to hear from them? Will they be conducting second-tier interviews? If you are interested and haven't heard, would they mind a phone call? Be sure to collect a business card with the name and phone number of your interviewer. On your way out, you might have an opportunity to pick up organizational literature you haven't seen before.

With the right preparation—a thorough self-assessment, professional clothing, and employer information—you'll be able to set and achieve the goals you have established for the interview process.

Interview Follow-Up

Quite often there is a considerable time lag between interviewing for a position and being hired or, in the case of the networker, between your phone call or letter to a possible contact and the opportunity of a meeting. This can be frustrating. "Why aren't they contacting me?" "I thought I'd get another interview, but no one has telephoned." "Am I out of the running?" You don't know what is happening.

Consider the Differing Perspectives

Of course, there is another perspective—that of the networker or hiring organization. Organizations are complex, with multiple tasks that need to be accomplished each day. Hiring is a discrete activity that does not occur as frequently as other job assignments. The hiring process might have to take second place to other, more immediate organizational needs. Although it may be very important to you, and it is certainly ultimately significant to the employer, other issues such as fiscal management, planning and product development, employer vacation periods, or financial constraints may prevent an organization or individual within that organization from acting on your employment or your request for information as quickly as you or they would prefer.

Use Your Communication Skills

Good communication is essential here to resolve any anxieties, and the responsibility is on you, the job or information seeker. Too many job seekers and networkers offer as an excuse that they don't want to "bother" the organization by writing letters or calling. Let us assure you here and now, once and for all, that if you are troubling an organization by over-communicating, someone will indicate that situation to you quite clearly. If not, you can only assume you are a worthwhile prospect and the employer appreciates being reminded of your availability and interest. Let's look at follow-up practices in the job interview process and the networking situation separately.

Following Up on the Employment Interview

A brief thank-you note following an interview is an excellent and polite way to begin a series of follow-up communications with a potential employer with whom you have interviewed and want to remain in touch. It should be just that—a thank-you for a good meeting. If you failed to mention some fact or experience during your interview that you think might add to your candidacy, you may use this note to do that. However, this should be essentially a note whose overall tone is appreciative and, if appropriate, indicative of a continuing interest in pursuing any opportunity that may exist with that organization. It is one of the few pieces of business correspondence that may be handwritten, but always use plain, good-quality, standard-size paper.

If, however, at this point you are no longer interested in the employer, the thank-you note is an appropriate time to indicate that. You are under no obligation to identify any reason for not continuing to pursue employment with that organization, but if you are so inclined to indicate your professional reasons (pursuing other employers more akin to your interests, looking for greater income production than this employer can provide, a different geographic location), you certainly may. It should not be written with an eye to negotiation, for it will not be interpreted as such.

As part of your interview closing, you should have taken the initiative to establish lines of communication for continuing information about your candidacy. If you asked permission to telephone, wait a week following your thank-you note, then telephone your contact simply to inquire how things are progressing on your employment status. The feedback you receive here should be taken at face value. If your interviewer simply has no information, he or she will tell you so and indicate whether you should call again and when. Don't be discouraged if this should continue over some period of time.

If during this time something occurs that you think improves or changes your candidacy (some new qualification or experience you may have had), including any offers from other organizations, by all means telephone or write to inform the employer about this. In the case of an offer from a competing but less desirable or equally desirable organization, telephone your contact, explain what has happened, express your real interest in the organization, and inquire whether some determination on your employment might be made before you must respond to this other offer. An organization that is truly interested in you may be moved to make a decision about your candidacy. Equally possible is the scenario in which they are not yet ready to make a decision and so advise you to take the offer that has been presented. Again, you have no ethical alternative but to deal with the information presented in a straightforward manner.

When accepting other employment, be sure to contact any employers still actively considering you and inform them of your new job. Thank them graciously for their consideration. There are many other job seekers out there just like you who will benefit from having their candidacy improved when others bow out of the race. Who knows, you might at some future time have occasion to interact professionally with one of the organizations with which you sought employment. How embarrassing it would be to have someone remember you as the candidate who failed to notify them that you were taking a job elsewhere!

In all of your follow-up communications, keep good notes of whom you spoke with, when you called, and any instructions that were given about return communications. This will prevent any misunderstandings and provide you with good records of what has transpired.

Job Offer Considerations

For many recent college graduates, the thrill of their first job and, for some, the most substantial regular income they have ever earned seems an excess of good fortune coming at once. To question that first income or to be critical in any way of the conditions of employment at the time of the initial offer seems like looking a gift horse in the mouth. It doesn't seem to occur to many new hires even to attempt to negotiate any aspect of their first job. And, as many employers who deal with entry-level jobs for recent college graduates will readily confirm, the reality is that there simply isn't much movement in salary available to these new college recruits. The entry-level hire generally does not have an employment track record on a professional level to provide any leverage for negotiation. Real negotiations on salary, benefits, retirement provisions, and so forth come to those with significant employment records at higher income levels.

Of course, the job offer is more than just money. It can be composed of geographic assignment, duties and responsibilities, training, benefits, health and medical insurance, educational assistance, car allowance or company vehicle, and a host of other items. All of this is generally detailed in the formal letter that presents the final job offer. In most cases this is a follow-up to a personal phone call from the employer representative who has been principally responsible for your hiring process.

That initial telephone offer is certainly binding as a verbal agreement, but most firms follow up with a detailed letter outlining the most significant parts of your employment contract. You may, of course, choose to respond immediately at the time of the telephone offer (which would be considered a binding oral contract), but you will also be required to formally answer the letter of offer with a letter of acceptance, restating the salient elements of the employer's description of your position, salary, and benefits. This ensures that both parties are clear on the terms and conditions of employment and remuneration and any other outstanding aspects of the job offer.

Is This the Job You Want?

Most new employees will respond affirmatively in writing, glad to be in the position to accept employment. If you've worked hard to get the offer and the job market is tight, other offers may not be in sight, so you will say, "Yes, I accept!" What is important here is that the job offer you accept be one that does fit your particular needs, values, and interests as you've outlined them in your self-assessment process. Moreover, it should be a job that will not only use your skills and education but also challenge you to develop new skills and talents.

Jobs are sometimes accepted too hastily, for the wrong reasons, and without proper scrutiny by the applicant. For example, an individual might readily accept a sales job only to find the continual rejection by potential clients unendurable. An office worker might realize within weeks the constraints of a desk job and yearn for more activity. Employment is an important part of our lives. It is, for most of our adult lives, our most continuous productive activity. We want to make good choices based on the right criteria.

If you have a low tolerance for risk, a job based on commission will certainly be very anxiety-provoking. If being near your family is important, issues of relocation could present a decision crisis for you. If you're an adventurous person, a job with frequent travel would provide needed excitement and be very desirable. The importance of income, the need to continue your education, your personal health situation—all of these have an impact on whether the job you are considering will ultimately meet your needs. Unless you've spent some time understanding and thinking about these issues, it will be difficult to evaluate offers you do receive.

More important, if you make a decision that you cannot tolerate and feel you must leave that job, you will then have both unemployment and self-esteem issues to contend with. These will combine to make the next job search tough going, indeed. So make your acceptance a carefully considered decision.

Negotiating Your Offer

It may be that there is some aspect of your job offer that is not particularly attractive to you. Perhaps there is no relocation allotment to help you move your possessions, and this presents some financial hardship for you. It may be that the health insurance is less than you had hoped. Your initial assignment may be different from what you expected, either in its location or in the duties and responsibilities that comprise it. Or it may simply be that the salary is less than you anticipated. Other considerations may be your official starting date of employment, vacation time, evening hours, dates of training programs or schools, and other concerns.

If you are considering not accepting the job because of some item or items in the job offer "package" that do not meet your needs, you should know that most employers emphatically wish that you would bring that issue to their attention. It may be that the employer can alter it to make the offer more agreeable for you. In some cases it cannot be changed. In any event the employer would generally like to have the opportunity to try to remedy a difficulty rather than risk losing a good potential employee over an issue that might have been resolved. After all, they have spent time and funds in securing your services, and they certainly deserve an opportunity to resolve any possible differences.

Honesty is the best approach in discussing any objections or uneasiness you might have over the employer's offer. Having received your formal offer in writing, contact your employer representative and indicate your particular dissatisfaction in a straightforward manner. For example, you might explain that while you are very interested in being employed by this organization, the salary (or any other benefit) is less than you have determined you require. State the terms you need, and listen to the response. You may be asked to put this in writing, or you may be asked to hold off until the firm can decide on a response. If you are dealing with a senior representative of the organization, one who has been involved in hiring for some time, you may get an immediate response or a solid indication of possible outcomes.

Perhaps the issue is one of relocation. Your initial assignment is in the Midwest, and because you had indicated a strong West Coast preference, you are surprised at the actual assignment. You might simply indicate that while you understand the need for the company to assign you based on its needs, you are disappointed and had hoped to be placed on the West Coast. You could inquire if that were still possible and, if not, would it be reasonable to expect a West Coast relocation in the future.

If your request is presented in a reasonable way, most employers will not see this as jeopardizing your offer. If they can agree to your proposal, they will. If not, they will simply tell you so, and you may choose to continue your candidacy with them or remove yourself from consideration. The choice will be up to you.

Some firms will adjust benefits within their parameters to meet the candidate's need if at all possible. If a candidate requires a relocation cost allowance, he or she may be asked to forgo tuition benefits for the first year to accomplish this adjustment. An increase in life insurance may be adjusted by some other benefit trade-off; perhaps a family dental plan is not needed. In these decisions you are called upon, sometimes under time pressure, to know how you value these issues and how important each is to you.

Many employers find they are more comfortable negotiating for candidates who have unique qualifications or who bring especially needed expertise to the organization. Employers hiring large numbers of entry-level college graduates may be far more reluctant to accommodate any changes in offer conditions. They are well supplied with candidates with similar education and experience so that if rejected by one candidate, they can draw new candidates from an ample labor pool.

Comparing Offers

The condition of the economy, the job seeker's academic major and particular geographic job market, and individual needs and demands for certain employment conditions may not provide more than one job offer at a time. Some job seekers may feel that no reasonable offer should go unaccepted for the simple fear there won't be another.

In a tough job market, or if the job you seek is not widely available, or when your job search goes on too long and becomes difficult to sustain financially and emotionally, it may be necessary to accept an inferior offer. The alternative is continued unemployment. Even here, when you feel you don't have a choice, you can at least understand that in accepting this particular offer, there may be limitations and conditions you don't appreciate. At the time of acceptance, there were no other alternatives, but you can begin to use that position to gain the experience and talent to move toward a more attractive position.

Sometimes, however, more than one offer is received, and the candidate has the luxury of choice. If the job seeker knows what he or she wants and has done the necessary self-assessment honestly and thoroughly, it may be clear that one of the offers conforms more closely to those expressed wants and needs.

However, if, as so often happens, the offers are similar in terms of conditions and salary, the question then becomes which organization might provide the necessary climate, opportunities, and advantages for your professional development and growth. This is the time when solid employer research and astute questioning during the interviews really pays off. How much did you learn about the employer through your own research and skillful questioning? When the interviewer asked during the interview "Do you have any questions?" did you ask the kinds of questions that would help resolve a choice between one organization and another? Just as an employer must decide among numerous applicants, so must the applicant learn to assess the potential employer. Both are partners in the job search.

Reneging on an Offer

An especially disturbing occurrence for employers and career counseling professionals is when a job seeker formally (either orally or by written contract) accepts employment with one organization and later reneges on the agreement and goes with another employer.

There are all kinds of rationalizations offered for this unethical behavior. None of them satisfies. The sad irony is that what the job seeker is willing to do to the employer—make a promise and then break it—he or she would be outraged to have done to him- or herself: have the job offer pulled. It is a very bad way to begin a career. It suggests the individual has not taken the time to do the necessary self-assessment and self-awareness exercises to think and judge critically. The new offer taken may, in fact, be no better or worse than the one refused. You should be aware that there have been incidents of legal action following job candidates' reneging on an offer. This adds a very sour note to what should be a harmonious beginning of a lifelong adventure.

PART TWO

THE CAREER PATHS

5

Introduction to the Business Career Paths

The chapters that follow are viable options for business undergraduate degree candidates. These career paths have been selected, investigated, and written with an eye to a candid appraisal of the job market for business majors with limited experience and an appreciation that no job is forever. Whatever employment decision you choose to make after college, think about acquiring specific skills quickly to ensure not only that you stay valuable to the job market but also that you can move from job to job because the skills you have obtained work well in many different employment settings.

Sales

Not only is sales a logical place to begin this part, it is also a solid beginning to many careers. Sales justifiably claims to be the "world's oldest profession" because sales are so crucial to commerce. Sales work generates the income that sustains all the other important activities of a business, including research and development, product testing, consumer research, packaging, and so on.

The sales force is a vital link between the consumer of a product and the manufacturer of that product. The consumer might be the faculty at an institution of higher learning, building service workers in a hospital, the purchasing agent for a manufacturing plant, or the proverbial person on the street. Sales representatives "represent" the organization—they speak for the organization and are the personification of the organization for most customers.

When you work in sales, you acquire skills that you will use for the rest of your working career. Of course, you will learn a great deal about people and how to best communicate with various folks. But the most valuable people skill you'll learn in sales will surprise you: listening. It's not accurate, however, to think that sales has a special corner on teaching you how to make presentations. Every career path in the book will help you improve your interpersonal skills. Sales may just do it faster and with more intensity.

Sales work will teach you about products, how they are manufactured, packaged, shipped, distributed, and presented to the final consumer. You'll learn to analyze the features and aspects of a product, to realize the multiple uses and dimensions possible for various goods and services. These are skills you will be able to apply to any future employment situation you find yourself in. When you can break a product or a service down into multiple aspects, you discover new ways to market and advertise that product or service to new and different segments of the buying public. Sales offers significant opportunities for developing creative thinking skills.

Sales work also teaches the value of everyone in an organization. This understanding will serve you well in future leadership or management roles. For example, you will learn to appreciate the telephone receptionists who are able to convey to your customer the professionalism of your firm through the efficiency and dispatch of their call handling. The shipping clerk who stays that extra minute to get a package ready for early departure the next morning has a direct influence on how you—the salesperson—are treated on your next call to the firm that received the order so promptly. The accounts department whose bills are on time and easy for customers to understand, even the janitorial staff that maintains the home office as a place that reflects your customer's good choice; the sales staff soon learns the value of each member of the organization to their success.

Sales is first among the paths because it is also the easiest career to access. Of course, employment in the top sales firms like those listed in *The 100 Best Companies to Sell For* are very competitive. Nevertheless, the reality is that as a new graduate, sales jobs are everywhere. Sales recruiters are common at job fairs and in campus recruiting offices, and sales want ads are frequent in newspapers advertisements.

Exactly who that "ideal" sales candidate might be remains a mystery, even to those doing the hiring. If you were to put a number of professional sales recruiters together in a room to discuss what constitutes a "strong" candidate for a sales job—get ready to hear a heated debate!

Energy, curiosity, creativity, and an ability to connect with people in an authentic way are generally accepted as essential ingredients for a salesperson. Beyond that, things get hazy. You see, sales can be inside, where customers come to you; outside, where you travel to your customers; or telemarketing, where everything is done by phone. So sales holds phenomenal potential for all types of individuals, including those who might think themselves too "shy" for a sales job. Additionally, sales can accommodate individuals with physical disabilities with less difficulty than many other professions.

The ease of entry is deceptive because the turnover is high. Sales is hard work. But for the new graduate who wants a job and is willing to work hard, sales work provides wonderful rewards: the highest incomes; oftentimes the nicest package of benefits, including vehicles; expense accounts; and very challenging assignments. No matter where you go after sales, you are likely to take away a legacy of polished interpersonal skills, problem-solving abilities, an appreciation of the team concept in a work setting, and a deeper and richer understanding of market concepts.

Retailing

Retailing comes next on the career pathway because of its dominance on the landscape. It is perhaps the sector of the economy that you have been most aware of and become most appreciative of as a consumer. The inside story is as exciting as a dramatic window display. Retailing is vital, dynamic, filled with risk and opportunity.

Though retailing has traditionally not placed a high value on education per se, its executive suites are heavily populated with business graduates. They arrived there, not by virtue of their diplomas, but by having assembled solid track records of success on the selling floor and through a succession of department assignments, using an understanding and appreciation of the market they serve, managing the risk factors of the decisions they make, and thoughtfully analyzing and reviewing sales performance for future decision making.

In retailing, the spotlight is on you the individual. Though many retailing organizations are justifiably termed conglomerates, even the biggest are structured as many smaller businesses, and individuals in retailing at any level have opportunities to take charge. Taking charge means making decisions and handling the consequences of those decisions. Retailing is not for the faint of heart.

It's ironic that this book may be your first serious introduction to retailing, which is often sadly neglected in business curricula—ironic because it is a career path that will exercise almost every academic course you've taken in your college studies. Retailing is the pulse of the nation, and to do retailing well, you need to have high levels of general information. All those liberal arts courses you wondered why you had to take will come in very handy in a retailing career when you are asked to provide items for sale to all kinds of people, from sports enthusiasts to dieters to three-year-old girls to retirees. You'll be grateful for your philosophy, sociology, psychology, and other general education courses, including foreign language training.

Retailing may be about providing people with goods and services they need, but the skill in retailing comes in anticipating these needs in the quantities and at the price levels that will secure the most profit for your organization. Retailing is the art and science of predicting human behavior in a shopping situation, and you cannot do that successfully without mixing with the public.

Nobody stands on ceremony in retailing. Of the jobs listed in this book, retailing puts the least emphasis on hierarchy of work. Everyone in retailing pitches in and does what needs to be done to get stock unpacked and get it on the floor, displayed, and marked so consumers can buy it. This is how aspiring retail executives learn what customers do, how they act and react to the selling situation. You can't make good retailing decisions from an office high above the selling floor. You need to get down behind a counter, roll up your sleeves, and talk to the customers, and then watch what they do.

No matter what happens in your career history after retailing, you gain an economist's view of market forces, for retailing is remarkably influenced by politics, weather, interest rates, and many other factors, large and small, that together give you the whole picture of how the economy works.

You learn in retailing how to put together a package that appeals to the public, price it, advertise it, merchandise it, and sell it. The ability to synthesize these elements can be utilized directly in countless other job situations, as a practitioner designing a trade show for manufacturers in the building trade or as an analyst serving on a consulting team advising a troubled business.

Most important, retailing teaches you how to make decisions. Retailing is about careful analysis, decision making involving risk, and data collection systems to provide the right kind of feedback necessary for future decision making. Whether you're in charge of a small section of the floor of a department store, a branch, or an entire building, retailing gives you enormous responsibility early in your career.

Health Care

Health care in the United States is currently in the throes of great change. The volatility and growth of the health-care industry make it a perfect time for you as a business graduate to enter the field. Because it is a specialized and technical field, you may not have considered it. One of the goals of this book is to give you strategies to transform your credentials from a general business degree to specific marketable talents and techniques. Getting in on the ground floor of health care will accomplish that.

Moreover, health care's changing climate will provide more opportunities than other paths in this book for job advancement, for as the industry shifts, realigns, consolidates, expands, and contracts, you will be given increased responsibility and increased opportunities to ride that growth while at the same time enhancing your own career.

Why are you attractive to health care? Watch the nightly news and read your local paper. You cannot avoid the constant barrage of news stories about the increasing conflict between the needs to contain escalating health-care costs and still maintain patient care and focus. Until the health-care industry began to undergo dramatic changes, the business side of health care was accomplished and maintained by homegrown professionals. Now that the industry is under such economic stress, health-care organizations have realized the advantages of a solid business background and are willing to train businesspeople in the unique culture and vocabulary of the health world.

This is an industry that needs new systems, new ways of doing things, new kinds of jobs, and new methods of handling people and completing paperwork. One of the reasons why this is an exciting field to enter after graduating is that what you'll learn is usable in many other nonmedical settings. What health care is about is handling large numbers of people in a highly individualistic way, people who need expensive products delivered in the most cost-conscious and efficient manner. The applicability of that to the hospitality industry, travel and tourism, hotels, and other similar service industries is obvious and is just another reason to look seriously at health care.

You'll need a strong systems orientation in this industry, so your quantitative skills need to be good. But even more important is the need to couple your analytical ability with a deeply sensitive and compassionate understanding of the nature of your business and the various reasons people seek health care. This sensitivity is evident in waiting rooms built with booths and partitions designed for a measure of privacy for an emotional or anxious time. Having no partitions might make for a larger, but less caring, facility. It's this constant juggling between fiscal reality and human considerations that makes this field so fulfilling as a career entity.

Of the five career paths in this volume, health care is the most volatile right now, and careers in health care are the most subject to the kinds of shifts and changes this book is designed to help you with. Entering health care in patient administration, fiscal management, facility support, or any other area, you need to stay cognizant of what skills you are acquiring and could acquire. Though you may not take your medical terminology to another job, you will certainly use any computer software skills, systems design and analysis, strategic planning, and evaluative skills.

These talents are of inestimable value to any employer who is interested in staying competitive. It's the talent of bringing the "big picture" to bear on a particular operational entity, doing a needs assessment, and prescribing changes, if necessary. It's a talent you'll use all of your working life, and you can acquire it in the changing field of the health-care industry.

Nonprofit Organizations

Nonprofits will be the biggest surprise for the business major and, in a way, that's a sad comment. There are wonderful careers for business majors in the nonprofit world that can lead to a rewarding lifestyle. Moreover, nonprofits welcome the business major in a way for-profits do not, for the business major is still relatively rare as an applicant in the nonprofit world.

Nonprofit organizations have not been a big part of the business curriculum. One of the biggest reasons for that is that nonprofits do not make as big a marketing splash as their for-profit cousins. Their advertising is seldom as colorful, as sexy, as eye-catching, or as expensive. Most have a lower profile in the business world.

Of course the nonprofits do market themselves, because most nonprofits need the public support and contributions that marketing brings them. However, the nature of the marketing nonprofits do as well as the nature of their financial statements tend to be more conventional, less controversial, and not as dramatic an illustration for a professor to choose for a business textbook or classroom.

Sadly, business educators seem to value business practices only when profit is involved, and yet, from a business standpoint, managing and sustaining a nonprofit corporation using public support, donations, corporate gifts, and federal grants requires infinitely more resources, inventiveness, cost consciousness, and sheer business acumen than many more wasteful for-profit organizations. And it is done for a good cause!

In nonprofits, the cause or mission of the organization replaces the for-profit motivation of the dollar. Whether it's the homeless population or Bosnian refugees, infant nutrition in the Sahara or medical services for Eastern Europe, forestry conservation or animal rights, nonprofits are about something other than money. They have a goal, and if you believe in that goal (and you must, if you're going to do a good job and enjoy your work), then every day you are going to be able to use your business education in a dramatically uplifting and ennobling way.

If you've had a classic business education, you may be conditioned to wonder "What do I give up for this job?" The answer is you need give up nothing. Nonprofit career professionals have good incomes that are increasingly competitive, and, in the senior leadership positions of organizations, entirely competitive. Nonprofits understand the need to provide incomes and benefits that will enable workers to stay committed to the organization and its goals. They know lower turnover of staff improves the quality of the organization and its ability to achieve its aims.

Of all the career paths listed in this book, the world of nonprofits may present the longest and most consistently enriching path, for not only will nonprofits reward your longevity of employment with increased responsibility and the material rewards that accompany that, but as Jeremy Rifkin, the nonprofit activist and writer, suggests, nonprofits are the sector of the economy that may best weather the vicissitudes of a changing world and may be the last sector of the economy to be diminished.

Are the jobs in nonprofit organizations different in any way from those in for-profit organizations? No. Any type of position in for-profit organizations can also be found within the nonprofit sector, including every other career path discussed in this book. Nonprofits need accountants, managers, salespeople, administrators, computer specialists, marketers, advertising specialists, public relations agents, and publicity managers. The list is endless. Sure, budgets are often tighter, so you'll very likely learn better cost-control management and gain an appreciation for the possibilities of reaching goals without expansive budgets. Working in a zero-based budget model is, obviously, excellent training, no matter where your career takes you. It teaches you to make the most of what you have and to be judicious when you have more.

Nonprofits are not usually thought of as glamorous, but your work in nonprofits could take place in some of the most interesting cities in the United States or the world. You could find a job in Washington, D.C., or in Kuala Lumpur. You could work at a desk in New York City or on a boat in the Adriatic Sea. Additionally, the nonprofit culture is one of pluralism, for nonprofits tend to be less concerned with homogenization and standardization. Nonprofit organizations welcome many kinds of people with many different talents.

A Strategy for the M.B.A.

The final career path tempts you with a different option: graduate school, but with a twist. The M.B.A. is a different kind of graduate degree, because for many career business professionals, an M.B.A. is the terminal degree. The Ph.D. may be the final degree for academicians and theorists, but for working professionals, the M.B.A. is the degree of choice.

For an employer, the M.B.A. brings with it an expectation of experience and expertise. Men and women with M.B.A.s are expected to be worth their often considerably higher salaries because they have experience and specialized skills that can be put right to work. That sounds reasonable, right? So what's the problem?

The problem is that an M.B.A. program can be a place where new business undergraduates decide to hide until the job market gets better. They often think, "Not only will I avoid a tough job market, but I'll arrive back on the scene more valuable than ever." This is erroneous on a number of counts. Not only does the M.B.A. imply experience to potential employers, but the M.B.A. programs themselves are usually geared to experienced, older working professionals, leaving the younger inexperienced M.B.A. graduate with a credential on paper but nothing to back it up. Inexperienced M.B.A.s often end up with jobs that neither require a graduate degree nor make it, financially, worth the efforts they have made to obtain the degree.

Chapter 10 discusses how you can gain valuable analytical skills as a financial analyst or research associate and then return to graduate school for your M.B.A. You gain wonderful experience that will leave you fully prepared for the rigors of the very best M.B.A. programs. After completing your M.B.A., you are ready to reenter the market with the enhancement of your new degree and business experience that is valuable in its own right.

The idea of thinking about even a traditional move such as going to graduate school in this carefully considered way is the same strategy that underlies each of the five chapters that make up the career paths in *Great Jobs for Business Majors*. You want to make a productive, fulfilling life for yourself You want a return on the investment you've made in your undergraduate education. Most important, you want to be able to weather the storms of an increasingly uncertain economy by building a résumé of talents that will allow you employment flexibility for the rest of your working life.

6

Path I: Sales

In a business world where conditions change rapidly, one element remains constant: organizations need skilled and talented representatives to connect and communicate with customers to build new markets for their products and services.

The field of sales offers a ready hiring market that allows you access to employment immediately upon graduation and the opportunity to acquire specific product information and become an expert in your field. Additionally, your experience will offer you countless opportunities to learn and improve your interpersonal skills that will continue to be valuable assets throughout your entire professional life.

Salespeople must be adept at decision making and have excellent time management and self-direction skills. In addition, increasingly, professional salespeople are required to be technically astute in order to manage the sophisticated technology needed for customer contact and service provision. If you consider yourself to be more of a listener instead of a talker, a problem solver rather than a solution dictator, and a consultant rather than a high-pressure order taker, you will find that you'll definitely excel in this field.

A sales career will transform even the most broad-based of business majors into a real specialist in business affairs. You'll understand marketplace economics, consumer behavior, and organizational systems in a way never possible in the classroom. You'll also gain immeasurably in your ability to interact with individuals and groups in every type of setting. Sales is a jump start to a career in which recognition comes faster than in almost any other employment sector.

Setting the Record Straight

There's no question—sales is misunderstood as a career option. Sales certainly has had its share of image problems. In literature (*Death of a Salesman*), film (*Tin Men*), and real life, we have encountered salespeople whose personas resemble caricatures of the fictional snake-oil purveyor. The reality is far, far different for the college graduate. Students usually have one opinion of sales, generally not very positive. Employers have another view of sales, and that is that it is not only positive and necessary, but exciting, challenging, and highly attractive. Well, since many of these employers were college students themselves not too long ago, you figure it out!

Even among business majors, there is some reluctance about sales as a career, and many students have concerns about compensation, measures of performance, ethical issues surrounding product quality, and accuracy of sales information.

As a career counselor, I have the opportunity to meet and talk with professional salespeople throughout the year when they visit my campus to recruit, when I attend job fairs and professional conferences, and when I make site visits to employers. Some of these sales professionals are new college graduates themselves, others are mid-career veterans, and yet others are senior staff who have long years of experience. They represent a full spectrum of experience in the field. It's fascinating to hear them speak enthusiastically of the many personal and professional rewards that careers in sales have brought them. Without exception, they speak of the professional challenges of larger accounts, important presentations to management, exciting travel opportunities, superb professional development opportunities, and satisfying financial rewards. Most often, they speak of wonderful, interesting colleagues and business friends.

Most interesting is how they think of themselves. As a group, they are poised, professional, and comfortable in social situations. They would tell you, often as not, that a career in sales is the reason. Individually, they range from extroverted toastmasters to quieter, more scholarly types. Some are comfortable with large groups, others prefer one-on-one. Many think of their jobs as educational and informative, not persuasive and certainly not hard-sell. They are deeply respectful of the people that comprise their market and do not see them as easily manipulated.

Ask any successful salesperson, "What is the most important skill you have?" You might expect the answer would be "personal power" or "persuasiveness," maybe "the ability to overcome objections" or "product knowledge." While all these attributes of a salesperson have their place, the skill most successful salespeople say they value above all is the ability to listen.

Selling Through Problem Solving

Contrary to public opinion, the objective of sales—certainly sales as practiced by professionals with a college degree and working for a reputable firm—is not to make somebody buy your product.

An IBM salesperson describes it this way:

> *I see myself as a problem solver. I try to get inside and understand my customers' work, their needs, and their problems. I listen. After I've had an opportunity to think about it, I'll prescribe solutions to their problems. Those solutions will include my company's products, but sometimes I will recommend a competitor's product if that is better suited to the job. I'm in this job for the long haul and my belief is each time I sell only what the customers need, I build trust. The more trust I build, the less "selling" I have to do. If I continue to get good at what I do, I may never have to "sell" again.*

A Crucial Role for Both You and the Company

Beginning your career in sales offers considerable advantages, both professional and personal, as a career path. *Great Jobs for Business Majors* begins with the sales career path for the very simple fact that, for most businesses, the sales function is the only aspect of the business generating income.

To illustrate this, take an example you are familiar with—your own college. All those buildings, all that equipment, faculty and staff salaries, food and supplies are supported largely by tuition. Tuition comes to the college with each accepted applicant, and the admissions office is charged with recruiting and selecting those applicants. Recently, demographics have been such that with the number of college-age students down, competition has become quite fierce for eligible students. School overhead doesn't just disappear. The admissions office's role of selling the school to applicants is crucial to a college's success and prosperity.

In a business, everyone else is using up the income that the sales force has generated. In fact, some organizations go so far in emphasizing the importance of the sales force that they draw their organizational charts with sales at the top and the chief executive officer at the bottom.

What is it about the sales role that is crucial for the business major to know? Sales and sales professionals are crucial to an organization's longevity. Organizations that employ sales staff have an important or even vital sales function. You will have a difficult time reaching top management positions in a company dominated by a sales culture unless you come up through the ranks, from sales rep to regional manager and so on. It would be difficult, if not impossible, to maintain credibility in establishing salary guidelines for sales personnel, to develop new promotional pieces to be used by the sales force, or to appreciate the sales impact of a product's features and attributes unless you have been there yourself.

Definition of the Career Path

Let's identify some of the activities engaged in by salespeople. Of course, sales professionals are as varied as the women and men who take on those functions. How they do their job is highly individual; with top sales professionals, you'll often see a singular professional style that is not only highly idiosyncratic but also indulged and approved of by top management. Glancing over the following list of sales functions, you can immediately understand that this job is far more complex and sophisticated than popular myth would have it:

- Identifying and contacting prospective customers
- Anticipating needs and maintaining good relations with the existing customer base
- Designing and delivering sales presentations
- Keeping records/activity reports/sales performance records
- Tracking sales orders/delivery schedules and other details
- Handling complaints/returns when received
- Keeping an eye on the competition and reporting activity
- Learning about new products and mastering marketing strategies

This short list of duties emphasizes communications, as you would expect, but there are many other skills and attributes that are suggested by this list.

Let's identify and examine some of these other important skills and attributes close up.

Product Knowledge

It is generally held that there are two kinds of "power" a salesperson has in the sales exchange. One kind of power is referent power—the perceived interpersonal connection between the parties in the sales exchange (discussed below). The other kind of power is the salesperson's knowledge of the product being presented. Experts tell us that even if we don't personally care for particular salespeople, we appreciate those who obviously have an in-depth knowledge of their product.

This expert product knowledge comes about in a number of ways. You may be attracted to the position because you already know something about the product or field. Your employer will provide training. You will learn from sales colleagues about their successful techniques for communicating a product's attributes to the market. And you will learn from your customers, who will indicate those features and satisfactions they derive from your product. Though your product knowledge may be specific, your growing understanding of how to communicate a product's many features and advantages to a customer is a skill you will take with you.

Promotability

I know of one large banking corporation that requires all new executive hires to spend some time on the teller line. For those joining the firm with new M.B.A. degrees, working as a teller might seem to be not the best use of their talents. The senior management of this bank, however, long ago learned that unless lending officers, portfolio managers, and administrators had contact with the average customer, they would never understand the basic business of the bank.

In any organization that has a sales force, to begin work there is to understand the organization in a very concrete, specific way. In the sales force, you learn how the organization is perceived by the consumer. This is true whether you are an admissions representative for a college or selling industrial boilers. Customer contact and your understanding and appreciation of the demands of a sales job will be the foundation and source of your credibility and authority as you advance in your career. This position will serve as training for future outside sales and marketing opportunities.

Customer Knowledge and Contact

Sales is about meeting people—lots of people. Each of these persons has a different need and appreciation for your product. Most of the time you encounter your clients on the job. Since you have initiated the meeting, you will also encounter a variety of receptions, from a warm welcome to a glacial stare. It's going to be up to you and your sales skills to make these moments work. One way you'll learn to do this is by appreciating exactly what each customer wants. Is it service? Perhaps it's product quality. It might be dependability. Sometimes it's the lowest price available. When customers are busy, you soon learn to judge each as an individual, find out what that customer needs, and get down to business!

Communication Skills

A professional saleswoman I know is known for her buoyant, cheerful personality. It's not an act. She is genuinely a positive, happy person who displays incredible energy and vitality. People like her, and her customers enjoy and anticipate her bright, cheery disposition. But she has her thoughtful days, like we all do. She has learned that if she's in a reflective mood, people ask, "What's wrong? What's the matter?" Body language, including facial expression, becomes very important. Professional salespeople need to be very aware of how they're coming across, at all times.

Clients won't believe you're interested in them if you're looking at your watch or tapping your foot while they speak. Eye contact, your full attention, and the appropriate sounds and movements of affirmation and understanding convey the message "I'm listening to you!" Salespeople understand that communication is a complex business.

Sales is the art and science of communication. The communication is often about important issues such as product features, delivery dates, prices, conditions of sales, financing, etc. A miscommunication can result in far more costly problems than just a lost sale. It's important that both parties understand each other. Professional salespeople become adept at ensuring that their messages are correctly received and "decoded."

We've mentioned the importance of listening. Answering the client's concerns is also important. Ensuring that the client understands you can be accomplished through questioning, reframing and restating what you've said, and by writing things down. Who said salespeople were just great talkers? Salespeople need to be excellent writers, speakers, listeners, and nonverbal communicators!

Personal Attributes

Of course, talking to someone who is currently in sales or who has had sales experience is one of the best ways to begin to appreciate the career path and your suitability for it. Whenever I talk to people who are currently in sales or have enjoyed a sales job in their work history, they invariably speak of the personal skills that they gained from sales work. What are these personal gains and why are they so important? I've identified some of the most critical skills below and quoted from sales job announcements that refer to these skills as hiring criteria:

Poise. Meeting new people, ease in all social situations, and the ability to chat and make friends with a variety of people all develop unconscious poise and confidence in sales professionals. It stays with them throughout their careers, no matter where that may be. Many sales professionals refer to this as the great gift of a start in sales. One ad states, "The candidate must possess the ability to relate to engineers, end users, and contractors."

Ability to Handle Stress. Sales situations—any situations involving people and negotiations—will involve stress as well. A sales career teaches the kinds of planning and strategies necessary to anticipate and avoid stress and the social skills to define and minimize the tension of stress-producing situations. An ad puts it this way: "Enjoy working in a fast-paced, dynamic environment."

Time Management. Most sales positions demand exceptional time management. Learning which clients to call on during which times, deciding when to do your paperwork, determining how to best use drive and fly time, and strategizing your week, your month, and your year for best effect all develop excellent time management skills. Many senior executives, when asked how they can be so productive, respond, "I began in sales and learned to use my time effectively." According to one ad, a sales position "Requires excellent communication and time management skills."

Decision Making. Whether you're out on the road alone, in negotiations with a client, competing for a major account against a worthy adversary, or discovering new markets or sales opportunities, there will be a need to make decisions. A sales job puts a strong emphasis on the individual, and that's why the hiring process is often lengthy and complex. Managers know you will frequently be called upon to think for yourself and the good of the firm. You'll have your successes and your mistakes. Hopefully, you'll be supported from above in each instance and will learn from both. Your job in sales will continue to demand good decision-making skills, many times on the spot. One ad asks, "Are you an aggressive sales professional who knows how to think on your feet?"

Job Growth

There are as many different types of sales positions as there are individuals to fill them. Each job holds the potential for both personal and professional growth, to varying degrees. Each job also places different demands on the job holder in terms of work productivity, self-management, travel, professional relationships, and product knowledge.

This book emphasizes the changes occurring in the world of business and the need for workers to be ready to reposition for a job change or an employer change. To be in the best position to accomplish these likely-to-be-required moves during your work career, you'll need to pay attention to your skill acquisition. Hold each job up against your own list of criteria:

- Does this sales job give me skills I can take with me to a new position within the same organization or, if necessary, to a new job outside my organization?
- If I have to move from this position, how easily can I document my achievements?
- Does this position offer me opportunities to learn to use new skills, new techniques, and new business tools?
- How does this position allow me to connect with the larger organizational structure, and how often will I make those connections?

Let's begin the discussion on career paths for sales professionals by looking at the variety of jobs being advertised at the time this book was being written:

> **Wisconsin Sales Territories Available:** An accelerated program designed to give participants a thorough foundation in consumer goods sales and sales management in preparation for a career in field marketing management. Due to the decentralized nature of the alcoholic beverage industry, career assignments with this firm are as much involved with developing marketing strategy as they are in sales execution. Successful candidates will be mature, aggressive, results-oriented self-starters who possess both a strong sales personality and have demonstrated above-average leadership aptitude. A strong interest in a sales management career is a prerequisite for success with this firm. Our recruiting program is focused on graduating baccalaureate candidates in business.

This is certainly an aggressive advertisement because it emphasizes management and marketing grooming functions outside of sales. It suggests candidates for the sales position being advertised will need to be potential management material. It seems to subscribe to the old-fashioned theory of a sales personality being born, not made. Nevertheless, this job ad for an outside sales position emphasizes education and training to a significant degree. It also clearly emphasizes that hiring decisions will be based on potential for promotability to field management. The college business degree requirement is also consistent with these expectations of high standards. This is a demanding position with lots of exposure to top management and very likely excellent compensation.

College/Military Dormitory Furniture Sales: Customers nationwide for our hardwood furniture designed to meet specifications for these settings. This position requires you to work as part of a five-member team to plan and implement a marketing approach, use all media to communicate with customers, represent the company at trade shows, help independent reps to increase sales in their territories, and execute bid documents for institutional purchasing departments.

This is a combination inside sales (working from within your organization), outside sales (visiting clients at their places of business), and marketing position that involves a team approach to very large purchases of institutional furniture. These necessitate highly consultative sales presentations with modifications of product frequently required. Each sale is critical and may take significant time to consummate; client relations are critical. This position also offers opportunities to work in a team, to gain experience in advertising and other media, to plan and execute presentations at trade shows, and to learn the specifics of institutional buying—all highly portable skills.

Inside Sales and Service Representative: Handle PC software orders from our customers on the telephone. You will process orders on our AS/400 system and use PCs for other daily operations. You will need a B.S. in business or equivalent, and at least one year of prior customer service or inside sales experience and excellent communication skills, systems/PC familiarity, and strong desire to deliver excellent service.

This is an inside, technical sales job requiring significant product knowledge and superb communication skills. What often can be achieved easily face-to-face requires far different types of skills to succeed when the contact is by phone.

A Word About Product Classifications

There's a difference between selling furniture and insurance. It's not very different from the distinction between high-quality, gourmet take-out food and dinner in an elegant restaurant. Tables or take-out are both concrete, real products that can be judged on the composition of their ingredients, quality of the workmanship, raw materials, and skill in preparation. Using easily established criteria, the tangible products can be judged independently of the organization producing them.

Insurance and fine dining both have elements that are less easy to assess; qualities such as the security, safety, and stability of the corporation or, on the other hand, the elegance, atmosphere, and class of the restaurant are intangible and very much in the eye of the beholder. They are far more difficult to assign value to, for their importance varies with the customer and the customer's needs.

The selling of tangibles versus intangibles puts different demands on the salesperson and affects the dynamics of the sales presentation, the type of client, and even the nature of the client interaction. Selling a tangible product allows the interaction to focus on product suitability and product specifications (color, design, performance). The transaction tends to be crisper and more succinct. Buyer and seller interaction is focused on the product and its features. Tangibles are bought by a wide range of consumers, from the least sophisticated and educated to professionals.

Intangible sales involve a more complex dynamic between the salesperson and the buyer. More credibility and trust needs to be engendered, and all sorts of subtle cues come into play such as the appearance, vocabulary, and demeanor of the salesperson. The focus is on the interaction with the salesperson as much as on the product. For this reason the selection of salespeople for intangible product classes is more sophisticated and complex, and these saleseople need to be more creative and verbal.

Working Conditions

Sales jobs are plentiful, but as this chapter indicates, they vary widely in quality, professionalism, training provided, opportunities to interact with colleagues, compensation, and growth potential. When you are a new grad out on the market for a sales job, there's a temptation to look at all the sales jobs available, rationalize away any concerns you might have, and take the first one offered you.

Most of the window dressing for your first job as a college graduate can be very attractive and distracting. A month of classroom training at the home office with all living arrangements provided, a company car that can be employed for personal use as well, the best salary you've ever imagined, beautiful business cards, a handsome leather briefcase—the list goes on and on. It's hard to look beyond these very tangible proofs of your successful employment and judge this new job by any other measure.

There are, however, three aspects of most sales jobs that are so dominant that they serve to define the nature of the employment experience, and the reader would be well advised to consider his or her suitability for a sales position against these criteria. Go back to Chapter 1, "The Self-Assessment," and review what you learned about your personal traits, values, and skills. Measure what you've learned about yourself against the following three critical aspects of sales positions.

Degree of Sociability

Most people remark on how easily sales professionals talk to just about anybody. It's quite easy to explain. Despite the fact that their jobs emphasize connecting with people, most sales professionals work alone and their contact with others is fairly brief and intermittent. They spend quite a bit of time on their own and would tell you that you need to be comfortable with yourself to be good at sales.

Some sales jobs involve teams; others are inside sales jobs that place you in an office, surrounded by the same coworkers each day, colleagues whom you can get to know well. Think clearly about your own past experience and how well you can handle the degree of sociability or the demands of being alone presented by the sales jobs you are considering.

Nature of the Client Contact

In most sales jobs, the actual "selling" of a product is not as challenging as connecting with the client. There are basically two ways to see a client: an invitation through some sort of prescreening or pre-sales work that has the client requesting your visit, or the cold call, when you call on a client who may not yet be aware of your product or service but whom you believe might be a good prospect for it.

Whether being invited or inviting yourself is more appealing or more challenging to you has much to do with your personality. Your tolerance of risk, your ability to handle new situations, and your ease in making acquaintances will be good barometers of which situation would be best for you over the course of a career.

Productivity/Competitiveness

Sales is often repetitive. It's not a career where you can sit at home and rest on your laurels. For many in this profession, a success only motivates them to further achievement. This competitive drive may not be directed at others. In some organizations, sales staff are not aware of others' track records in the field. It may simply be a competition with yourself. Because sales always involves seeking new markets and new clients for products and services, that competitive spirit is essential.

This competitive drive can be hard to maintain if you are selling intangibles. For example, if you are working for a major pharmaceutical manufacturer talking to physicians about drug therapies and encouraging them to try your products, you cannot legally "sell" anything. You simply can stress advantages of your product and encourage the physician to prescribe the drug when indicated. Thus, it can be difficult to measure success when selling such intangibles. You might wonder at the end of the day "What have I accomplished?" Do you need to see an order sheet all filled out? Each of us has different needs for feeling successful, and a carefully chosen sales job can meet that need.

Training and Qualifications

People who hire for sales positions know best how difficult it is to predict who will do well in this profession. You may have little prior experience on which to judge your suitability and a sneaking suspicion that your sales technique classes in college may not have been as challenging as the "real thing."

Professional recruiters know all this. But they also know the demands of the marketplace and the sophistication and educational background of people you'll be meeting. They know that the increasing demands of sales automation require an ability to master the computer and to manage one's own time and workflow. They have found a college degree to be the best training ground for many of the demands of today's professional sales consultant.

Though you may have some natural ability for sales, you will need further training in sales skills. In addition, you will want to be provided with a structured opportunity to learn about the products and services you'll be selling. The best sales positions offer the greatest amounts of formal training. However, the training is not always provided before you begin selling. Some firms have their new sales recruits attend formal sales schools, complete with dormitories, exams, and classroom presentations before you meet the public. Other organizations have found training to be more worthwhile following a brief period of actual field sales, perhaps three to six months. The philosophy behind this decision is that some exposure to the demanding role of the sales professional will help you to appreciate the training and be more aggressive in your studies. Both philosophies have merit.

Be wary of those positions that ask you to fund yourself until you are paid, provide your own transportation, or offer no formal training. This kind of employment structure places no responsibility on the hiring organization. Consequently, rapid turnover (common in these jobs) is not very damaging to the organization since it has spent little money on each salesperson. A firm that invests in your training has invested in you and wants you to succeed.

Earnings

Sales offers the entry-level graduate the highest possible earnings available with a college business degree, with only a few exceptions for some technical majors. High earnings are attractive to many students who graduate with some debt burden and a strong motivation to begin to live on their own and make a life for themselves.

Positions in selling pay either a salary, a commission, or a combination of the two. (See Table 6.1.) As an entry-level salesperson, you will probably be more attracted to a salaried selling position. It seems less risky and seemingly puts less responsibility on you to produce than a commission system does. Straight-salary plans work best for employers when it is difficult for management to determine which person on the staff actually made the sale or when the product involved has a broad, cyclical sales pattern, which would leave the sales staff with virtually no income during the slow periods if commissions were involved.

TABLE 6.1 AVERAGE SALARY FOR SALES STAFFERS IN 2001

	Total Compensation	Base Salary	Bonus Plus Commission
Executive	$122,899	$87,178	$35,721
Top performer	$139,459	$78,483	$60,976
Mid-level rep	$77,179	$49,144	$28,035
Low-level rep	$51,992	$37,698	$14,294
Average of all reps	$80,023	$54,452	$25,571

Source: 2002 SMM/Equation Research survey of 2,644 sales and marketing executives. *Sales & Marketing Management*, May 2002.

Sales professionals who have gained skills and confidence in their abilities are often more attracted to commission plans. Commission plans offer them unlimited income if they are successful. Straight commission gives the greatest incentive to salespeople while maintaining a predictable sales cost in relation to sales volume. Two factors working against straight commissions are: (1) high turnover and burnout of sales staff and (2) a sales process tainted by the need of sales personnel to move product to pad the salesperson's paycheck regardless of a customer's true need for the product or service.

Consider compensation plans carefully, regardless of your financial needs. It can be very disheartening to leave a position because of a disagreement over the pay arrangements when a little forethought might have anticipated problems.

Combination plans exist with fixed salaries and incentive features added on. This builds continuity in the sales force, yet allows superior sales staff to shine, and it encourages everyone to develop more business.

The bouquet of roses of each pay scheme has its own thorns. A straight-salary job cannot reward superior achievement, and that may grow to be a frustration if you are exceptionally successful in your position. If you expect to be the best you can be, shouldn't your paycheck reflect that? With a straight-salary job, you and the poorest performer take home the same paycheck!

Commission rewards ability and performance, and that can be attractive to the confident sales pro. However, be sure you understand what the minimum performance levels are, how much you need to do to earn your commission, and how feasible those goals may be. What is the waiting period, following a successful sale, before you receive your compensation? Occasionally, when commission salespeople are "too" successful, an organization will redivide their territory and add sales staff. The philosophy behind that move is that if one individual can do so well, there may be even more opportunity if additional sales staff are employed. However, for the successful salesperson, this only means less territory and much harder work to realize the same income as before.

Commission is not as risky as most graduates think. If (and this "if" is important) the organization that hires you is spending money and time on your training, its sales managers do not want to see you fail and are taking steps to ensure you succeed. Their compensation plans are based on experience born of what past salespeople could do and what incentives they needed to do it. There is no success if salespeople drop out because they can't make any money. The organization would suffer and, ultimately, fail.

Benefits Are Important, Too

Take some time to review a book like *The 100 Best Companies to Sell For*, now out of print but still available, or *The 100 Best Companies to Work For*, or *High Performance Sales Organizations*, and develop a sense of the benefit packages offered by the best organizations. They will help give you a standard by which to judge your own package. Benefits are income when they apply to your educational progress, your medical or dental bills, or your need for a vehicle and insurance. A good benefit package is estimated at a third of your income, so if you are salaried at $30,000, your benefits can cost your employer another $10,000, depending upon your usage.

Some typical benefit items include:

- Medical/dental insurance
- Life insurance
- Pension plan
- Disability insurance
- Travel allowance
- Company car
- Profit sharing
- Stock purchase plan
- Child care
- Retirement plan
- Savings/investment plan
- Tuition assistance
- Relocation assistance
- Memberships (fitness clubs, etc.)

Career Outlook

Whatever volatility our economy is experiencing these days, sales jobs remain critical to a firm that needs to move its product on to the next stage in the channel of distribution. Everyone in that channel, from the originator of the product to the retail merchant, is seeking someone to buy what they themselves have just bought. The longer any channel member holds the product, the more risk that member engenders of perishability, fire, theft, obsolescence, loss of market value, encroachment by competitors, or failure to realize a profit.

Salespeople are critical in organizations of this kind because they generate that vital activity of moving the product on, making the profit, and reducing the risk of holding that product too long. Salespeople are not only the largest occupational group in the United States but the one with the largest projected number of new jobs in the coming decade. It's quite amazing to think about the sales process occurring for an infinite number of products to an infinite number of market segments of consumers. Somewhere in that sales cosmos is a market and product you would enjoy.

A Word About the "Marketing Contract"

College graduates like yourself are sometimes amazed at the vast array of products that are bought and sold in the marketplace, many of which you've never heard of, others seemingly objectionable and distasteful to anyone. Who buys this stuff? The answer is quite simple.

The marketing contract says that if the public demands a product, channels will exist to distribute that product and purveyors will appear who will stock and sell that product. That explains not only all the different carbonated beverages in a supermarket aisle but also the booming trade in pornography or drugs. Products do not stay in the market if there is no demand. As a salesperson, you will find—if you do any kind of research or exploration—that there is an incredible array of goods and services, tangible and intangible, available on the marketplace, and one of these will demand your particular talents and skills. Go out and find it!

Strategy for Finding the Jobs

There's something interesting about the hiring of sales personnel that's different from the hiring of other kinds of professionals. With accountants, analysts, purchasing agents, or administrative support, the employer looks for professionalism in the résumé and cover letter but is more interested in finding out what the job candidate knows, what his or her experience has been, and whether the candidate seems adequately prepared for the job under consideration.

In the sales personnel market, every aspect of the coming together of the candidate and potential employer is a clue to the candidate's potential in a sales job. What better exercise in persuasiveness is there than the job search? Can you think of any other activity that puts as much emphasis on the kind and quality of one's communication as the job search and the interview itself? A job search is by and large a sales exercise, and if you wish to become a sales professional, an employer has every right to expect to see the beginnings of brilliance in how you go about seeking your job! Consider the following factors:

The Significance of the Résumé and Cover Letter

All sales jobs involve some degree of written communication. In fact, it's probably a fair corollary that the more important or senior the sales position, the more it will involve written proposals, presentations, and projects. Early signs of a salesperson's professionalism might be the résumé and cover letter. Do they:

- Get to the point?
- Interest and excite the reader?
- Look attractive and distinctive?
- Display the hallmarks of attention to detail and accuracy?

It is no exaggeration to say that résumé and cover letter readers have every right to expect that if you cannot put together a perfect sales package for yourself, you won't be able to do it for them, either.

When executives have only a day to devote to interviewing and they must reduce a pile of two hundred résumés and cover letters to eight to ten candidates, the first ones to go in the wastebasket are those that have typographical errors, or look confusing or "tricky" with too many typefaces or overly fancy graphics. "Gee, the candidate must not have proofed this work. Poor attention to detail. I wouldn't want something like that going out under our letterhead." And out it goes!

The Unique Importance of the Interview for Sales

For a sales position, the key to being hired is the interview, for it is the most obvious early demonstration of your communication facility at presenting a product (yourself) and ability to make a winning case for your employment. Even acknowledging your newness at interviewing and the anxiety of most new college grads during interviews, most recruiters will still want and expect to see some nascent indications that you have what it takes. If you're shy and retiring or fail to demonstrate your skills, you'll disappoint your interviewer. If you are overly confident, a braggart, or loud and pushy, you'll turn your interviewer off.

Try to balance the interview as best you can. Try to give as much information as you get, and answer questions with pertinent and persuasive information. If the interviewer ends up doing all the talking, he or she learns nothing about you, and if you do all the talking, you miss a great opportunity to learn more about the organization.

Sales is about communication, but sometimes that communication is not just about the product or service you are selling. Interviewers, accordingly, will want to know what you're reading, your opinion on current events, and your views on national legislative issues. Salespeople need to be well read and have high levels of general information, for they will need to draw on that each day as they communicate with a diverse range of customers.

The Telephone Interview for Sales

When sales work involves the telephone or when a firm needs to screen a large number of applicants, the telephone interview as a first-stage interview technique is helpful and inexpensive for employers. Some important tips for sales candidates in the phone interview include:

• Arrange to take the interview where you will not be disturbed and where background noise will be at a minimum. You don't want to miss any information, nor do you want the interviewer to be distracted by background noise.

• Have a large writing surface near the phone and try to note as much of the information being given as possible. It'll come in handy later. Don't be shy about asking to have important details repeated or to ensure you have the correct spelling of a name.

• Speak very clearly and distinctly into the mouthpiece. Don't let your responses go on and on. When you've finished a response, it should be clear to the listener.

• Most of all, try as best you can to let your voice express its natural warmth. Be yourself and be as natural and as relaxed as a job interview situation allows. Using your facial muscles to smile when thinking about a question or expressing pleasure is a technique many successful phone speakers find helpful in conveying emotions through the voice.

The Personal Interview for Sales

The key word here is *appearance*. Your first impression is largely determined by how you look. Your interviewers know the impression you make on them is basically the impression you'll be making on the organization's clients and potential customers. Many, many salespeople are selected in large part for their personal appearance. It's called *referent power*, and it is the ability of clients or customers to relate to the salesperson as someone of their standing, background, or education.

Possible Employers

Sales jobs of every type and description seem to be everywhere. In fact, many other kinds of job seekers complain that sales jobs are all they ever see. Each sales job describes itself differently, and each job description seems to focus on a different aspect of the position. For some it's customer contact, for others it's product knowledge, and yet others emphasize productivity or profit margin. How do you judge what's best for you?

Make a list of what you want in a sales position. We all want different things, so list your requirements. Perhaps financial security is number one on your list. Then you need to be on the lookout for those sales jobs that offer a salary and avoid commission status. Perhaps you want to further your education and want additional training. Seek out those sales positions advertising training programs or emphasizing high-quality professional development for the sales force. Other priorities might be travel, activity level, productivity, income production, calling on established clients, or making cold calls on prospective clients. Whatever it is, you need to draw up your own working list of elements you're seeking in a sales position so you can adequately judge and compare the market offerings.

Begin with the best and establish your own criteria. Start with a reference work such as *The 100 Best Companies to Sell For* and learn the particulars of the sales job from the crème de la crème of sales organizations. This book will give you valuable insight into:

- Entry-level salaries for sales
- Senior-level salaries for sales
- Products and services offered by each company
- Benefits (including bonuses, perks, etc.)
- Corporate culture and style
- Training—which firms stress formal training programs and which emphasize on-the-job experience
- An in-depth discussion of the firm and the role of sales in the organization
- Criteria used in selecting sales candidates

Now that you have drawn up a list of your criteria and you have read about and understood the criteria of the best in the business, you should begin the process of applying for the jobs that seem to meet your needs.

Sales jobs are widely advertised and recruited because hiring firms often have to talk with and screen a number of candidates before they find one that fits their needs. You will have to do the same in your search. For that reason, the job search for sales is a busy one with lots of résumé mailing, telephone interviewing, job lead follow-up, and cold-calling before you "connect" with that perfect job. Some of the best places to look are described in the following paragraphs.

Your college career office will not only contain numerous subscriptions to job posting newsletters offering entry-level sales jobs, but is also on the mailing list of many employers who look on college campuses to fill sales jobs, especially in the spring. Your career office can direct you to resources that you might otherwise never discover. For example, *2002 Sports Market Place* directory (see Additional Resources) contains thousands of sales positions in sporting equipment and sports-related products and services. Visible Ink's *Marketing and Sales Career Directory* (Detroit, Gale Group) is another rich source of employers seeking sales candidates.

Large metropolitan newspapers are excellent sources for sales jobs, especially Sunday editions. Check them out every week.

Job fairs come in all varieties, specializing in many kinds of jobs. The sales job fair is one of the most common types. These provide a good way to distribute your résumé, meet lots of employers, practice your stand-up interviewing skills, and check out the competition.

Informal or formal college alumni networks are a fine way to tap into the hidden job market. You'll still need to be on your toes in the job search, but alumni contacts can give you the inside track to unadvertised job openings.

The Internet is another valuable resource. Hit the websites of the companies you have targeted as your preferred employers. Then, to see what's being advertised, search under "sales" at the mega-job websites. Look into your area of specialization, too, if you are focusing on medical or pharmaceutical sales, say, or technical sales. Industry associations often have job links to good sites.

Possible Job Titles

The sales industry itself works very hard to improve the professional standing of its salespeople and move them out from under any stigmatizing labels or job titles that might inhibit their abilities to do their jobs. So you'll see several titles listed below that don't even contain the word *sales*. Get used to that in seeking out sales positions. It may be your first signal that the hiring organization has paid particular attention to the role of its sales force.

Account executive	Product line manager
Account representative	Product manager
Area director	Regional manager
Area manager	Sales director
District manager	Sales manager
Major account representative	Salesperson
Market representative	Sales representative
National sales manager	Sales specialist
Outside sales representative	Service representative

Related Occupations

The skills you've acquired in sales tend to be rather universally esteemed: listening, speaking, public presentation, decision making, time management, product specification knowledge, and an ability to "connect" with people authentically and quickly. Sales professionals can easily adapt to a wide variety of occupations. A sampling would have to include the following:

Advertising	Produce management
Career counseling	Promotions
Chambers of commerce	Public relations
Communications	Real estate
Consulting	Trade fair design
Manufacturer's representative	Training and development
Marketing management	Travel agent

Professional Associations

American Business Women's Association
9100 Ward Pkwy., P.O. Box 8728
Kansas City, MO 64114-0728
(800) 228-0007
Fax: (816) 361-4991
abwa@abwahq.org

American Marketing Association
311 S. Wacker Dr., Suite 5800
Chicago, IL 60606
(800) AMA-1150
Fax: (312) 542-9001
marketingpower.com
Members/Purpose: Professional society of marketing and marketing research executives, sales and promotion managers, advertising specialists, academics, and others interested in marketing.
Publications: *American Marketing Association—Proceedings, International Membership Directory, Journal of Health Care Marketing.*

Association of Incentive Marketing
1620 Route 22
Union, NJ 07083
(908) 687-3090
Members/Purpose: Conducts education and information programs to improve the effectiveness of incentive merchandising through the influence of the professional incentive executive.
Publications: *Incentive Casebook: How Marketers Motivate, Association of Incentive Marketing—Incentive Report, Association of Incentive Marketing Membership Directory.*

Association of Sales Administration Managers
P.O. Box 1356
Lawrence Harbor, NJ 08879
(732) 264-7722
asamnet@aol.com
Members/Purpose: Seeks to resolve problems with production, distribution, sales services, employment, and internal financial functions.

Bureau of Wholesale Sales Representatives
1100 Spring St. NW, Suite 700
Atlanta, GA, 30309
(800) 877-1808
bwsr.com
Members/Purpose: Salespeople of wholesale women's, men's, and children's apparel and accessories, shoes, toys, and Western wear and equipment.
Publication: *Bureau News.*

Direct Selling Association
1275 Pennsylvania Ave. NW, Suite 800
Washington, DC 20004
(202) 347-8866
dsa.org
Members/Purpose: Manufacturers and distributors selling consumer products door-to-door, by appointment, and through home-party plans.
Training: Offers specialized education.
Publications: *Direct Selling World Directory, International Bulletin, Membership Directory, News from Neil, Who's Who in Direct Selling.*

Hospitality Sales and Marketing Association International
8201 Greensboro Dr., Suite 300
McLean, VA 22102
(703) 610-9024
Fax: (703) 610-9005
hsmai.org
Members/Purpose: An international organization devoted entirely to education of executives employed by hotels, resorts, and motor inns.
Training: Conducts seminars, clinics, and workshops.
Publications: *Directory, Marketing Review, Update.*

Life Communicators Association (LCA)
P.O. Box 196
Zionsville, IN 46077
lcaonline.org
Members/Purpose: Encourages the interchange of experience and ideas. Advertising, sales promotion, public relations, and company communications specialists of life insurance companies. Meets jointly with Insurance Marketing Communications Association (IMCA).
Training: Conducts workshops to aid in educational development of junior members.
Publications: *Life Communications*, membership roster.

National Association of Publishers Reps
P.O. Box 3139
New York, NY 10163
(212) 685-3254
naprassoc.com
info@naprassoc.com

Members/Purpose: Independent publisher's representatives selling
advertising space for more than one publisher of consumer, industrial,
and trade publications.
Publications: *Bulletin*, roster of members.

National Society of Pharmaceutical
Sales Trainers (formerly Society of
Pharmaceutical and Biotech Trainers)
5 Homestead Ln.
Avon, CT 06001-2933
(860) 675-1824
spbt.org
Members/Purpose: Seeks to improve professionalism within the field by
raising standards of development and training programs; encourages
members' self-development by facilitating information exchange.
Training: Conducts workshops annually.
Publications: *Newspost*, roster.

Pi Sigma Epsilon
427 East Stewart St.
Milwaukee, WI 53207
(414) 328-1952
Fax: (414) 328-1953
pse@pse.org
Members/Purpose: Professional fraternity—marketing, sales management,
and selling.
Publications: *Convention Update, Dotted Lines, Headquarters Bulletin,
Journal of Personal Selling and Sales Management.*

Professional Society for Sales and
Marketing Training
180 N. LaSalle St., Suite 1822
Chicago, IL 60601
(312) 551-0SMT (0768)
Fax: (312) 551-0815
smt.org
smt@rmygroup.com
Members/Purpose: Corporate managers and directors of training, sales and
marketing, and human resources development.

Promotion Marketing Association
of America (PMAA)

257 Park Ave. S, 11th Floor
New York, NY 10010
(212) 420-1100
pmalink.org

Members/Purpose: Promotion service companies, sales incentive organizations, and companies using promotional programs. Supplier members are manufacturers of premium merchandise, consultants, and advertising agencies.

Training: Sponsors seminars.

Publications: *Outlook, PMAA Membership Directory, Promotion Marketing Abstract.*

Promotional Products Association
International

3125 Skyway Cir. N
Irving, TX 15038-3526
(972) 252-0404
ppai.org

Members/Purpose: Promotes industry contacts in thirty countries. Suppliers, distributors, and direct selling houses of specialty advertising including calendars, imprinted specialties, and executive gifts.

Training: Holds executive development and sales training seminars.

Publications: *Specialty Advertising Association International—Membership Directory and Reference Guide, Specialty Advertising Business.*

Radio Advertising Bureau (RAB)

261 Madison Ave., 23rd Floor
New York, NY 10016
(212) 681-7200
rab.com

Members/Purpose: Membership includes radio stations, radio networks, station sales representatives, and allied industry services, such as producers, research firms, schools, and consultants. Exhorts advertisers and agencies to promote the sale of radio time as an advertising medium.

Publication: *RAB Instant Background: Profiles of 50 Businesses.*

Sales Association of the
Paper Industry
P.O. Box 2718
Darien, CT 06820
(203) 656-3307
Members/Purpose: Sales, marketing, advertising, and sales promotion
personnel for primary producers of pulp, paper, and paperboard.
Training: Sponsors seminars and meetings with speakers on special
subjects.
Publications: *Bulletin, Directory of Members.*

Sales and Marketing Executives
International (SMEI)
P.O. Box 1390
Sumas, WA 98295-1390
(800) 999-1414
smei.org
smei@earthlink.net
Members/Purpose: Seeks to make overseas markets more accessible by
interchange of selling information and marketing techniques with
executives in other countries.
Training: Sponsors seminars, conducts career education programs, offers
Graduate School of Sales Management and Marketing at Syracuse
University, New York.
Publications: *Marketing Times, SMEI Leadership Directory.*

The Society for Marketing
Professional Services
99 Canal Center Plaza, Suite 250
Alexandria, VA 22314
(800) 292-7677
Fax: (703) 549-2498
smps.org
Members/Purpose: Employees of architectural, engineering, planning,
interior design, landscape architectural, and construction management
firms who are responsible for the new business development of their
companies.
Training: Provides specialized education through regional seminars held
two to three times a year.
Publications: membership roster, *SMPS Marketer.*

Women in Advertising and Marketing
4200 Wisconsin Ave. NW, Suite 106–238
Washington, DC 20016
(301) 369-7400
wamdc.org
Members/Purpose: Professional women in advertising and marketing in
Washington, D.C. Serves as network to keep members abreast of
developments in advertising and marketing.
Publications: membership directory, newsletter.

Women in Direct Marketing International
224 Seventh St.
Garden City, NY 11530
(516) 746-6700
wdmi.org
Members/Purpose: Seeks to advance the interests and influence of women
in the direct response industry; provides for communication and career
education; assists in the development of personal career objectives; and
serves as a professional network to develop business contacts and foster
mutual goals.
Training: Sponsors monthly seminar, workshops, and summer internship
program.
Publications: *Women's Direct Response Group—Membership Roster, Women's
Direct Response Group—Newsletter.*

Women in Sales Association
8 Madison Ave.
Valhalla, NY 10595
Members/Purpose: Promotes professional development of women in sales.
Provides opportunities to establish business contacts and to share
information and ideas.
Training: Conducts work sessions on topics; sponsors career guidance
workshops.
Publications: membership directory, *Sales Leader.*

7

Path 2: Retailing

Retailing is the sale of selected merchandise directly to the consumer. Though this definition of retailing might be satisfactory for a business exam, in actuality retailing defies description! Retailing is an exciting career with enough change and excitement to keep you fascinated and on your toes for the life of your career. But retailing can also be a doorway through which you can enter the worlds of fashion, sales, product management, or training and development. The majority of today's top managers in these fields began their careers in training programs offered by the retailers that were their very first employers after graduation.

Dramatic changes are taking place in the world of retailing. Let's examine a few examples of this marketing revolution and what those changes mean for the business major looking for a dynamic and fast-paced career opportunity.

E-retailing, or online retailing, opens up a whole new channel for commerce. It's not clear yet how far this trend will go. It looks as though most companies will choose a multichannel approach, rather than a pure online presence; the virtual marketplace is still a few years away. In 2002, the pioneers in retailing through the Internet were just beginning to see some profits materialize, after a long initial period of investment and operating at a loss. But most observers are counting on E-commerce to keep growing in the future.

Another trend is apparent in the tie-ins between entertainment and retailing. Motion picture and television companies, seeking incremental income and enhanced brand image, are increasingly opening branded-merchandise stores. Disney operates 615 specialty stores in nine countries. Viacom operates theme parks and retail video stores through its retail and recreation division, Paramount Parks, and 7,800 Blockbuster video stores.

We have at least two critical clues here to the importance of retailing in the American marketplace. Major corporations such as Disney and Viacom realize that for reaching the public, retailing is a worthwhile investment in capital expenditure, training and development, and hiring of expertise. Organizations are beginning to see retailing as the important "missing link" in their presentation of a complete array of goods and services. In today's competitive arena, many business enterprises appear to want more direct contact with the consumer.

You can see from the examples above that it isn't enough to just know your product. The career-minded retail professional must stay abreast of demographic trends such as population shifts, new technology, and changing lifestyles. Retailing often is on the cutting edge of technology. Retail stores were the first to use fashion/music videos on continuous loop on the sales floor to stimulate customer awareness and interest in apparel products. These tapes were early forerunners of music videos. Retailers were the first to sell in cyberspace and will be the first to use virtual reality to let shoppers "try on" clothes or experience home furnishings or outdoor equipment, and so on.

Manufacturers hoping to differentiate their brands from private-label brands are increasingly opening their own retail outlets. Footwear maker Dr. Martens, for example, opened a department store in London's Covent Garden district. The store, in addition to selling boots and shoes, sells branded gift items and provides services. The company hopes to create a lifestyle brand.

The concept of forward integration, manufacturers controlling the retailing of their own products, is an increasingly common phenomenon. It is another dramatic signal to business majors that retail is not only important, but getting bigger and bigger. The idea has obvious merit. If manufacturers really care about their shoes or clothes or ski equipment, what could be better than creating their own stores, with a complete line of their products and retail salespeople specially trained by them to display the products and educate the public in a way not possible with retail employees who must learn about and sell a huge array of products.

Wal-Mart Stores opened an environmentally friendly "eco-store." The store, which carries Wal-Mart's standard merchandise assortment, has beams made of wood instead of steel, skylights that provide natural light, and a chlorofluorocarbon-free air-conditioning system. The store has a recycling theme and an on-site recycling center. It became a source of ideas for Wal-

Mart's expansion program. The company also helps fund local recycling programs and environmental education activities. Analysts predict that other retailers will adopt such concepts.

Stores responding so dramatically to the public's concern with the environment is but one example of the changes that constantly alter the face of retailing in today's marketplace. Retailing is the pulse of the public. If you want to know what the American public values, where their interests lie, how they play or dress, what they read, eat, or buy, just visit a store! And as the public's interests change, often overnight, retailing is the first to respond.

Retail stores and shopping malls are facing a variety of competition, ranging from superstores to video shopping, and are countering by introducing entertaining into their retail plans. The Mall of America contracted with Knotts Berry Farm to provide a central amusement core in this, the largest mall in the United States. Some malls are also offering more refined amenities such as museums, schools, and even churches.

Retailing is no place for the amateur or for the faint of heart. It's a world that demands you take a risk, for only the strong survive. One reason why the business graduate is a welcome candidate for jobs in the retail sector is the constant, unrelenting competition demanding a variety of skills, decision-making ability, and solid business education.

The number of earth stores, retailers selling environmentally friendly products, in the United States grew from virtually zero in 1990 to about two hundred in 1993, according to *Green Marketing Alert* editor Carl Frankel. By now it's a nationwide phenomenon. Retailers such as Earth Mercantile, Earth General, Restore the Earth Store, Terre Verde, and Eco-Wise can be found in most regions of the country. Frankel estimates that earth-store revenues reached about $28 million in 1992. Many other stores—and websites—adopted the green retailer theme by the 2000s. Several "green retailing" stores in almost every state are listed at ecolivingcenter.com. Others such as Real Goods operate as both storeowners (Hopland, California) and catalog retailers. Real Goods sends out 4 million catalogs annually.

It could be environmentally related products; it could be angels, quilting materials, or mountain gear. The point here is the trend toward narrow focus and "boutique" concepts in retailing. No longer do retailers try to do everything for everybody. What people want now is someone targeting a narrow market with specific products that have an appeal to the aware consumer, be it coffee or clothing. But there's a lot of risk here. If you're just putting brown eggs in your basket to sell, you'd better be sure that there's a strong, continuing market for brown eggs!

Was Retailing Missing from Your Business Curriculum?

A common reason for making poor career choices is lack of information about all the possibilities. Though retailing careers continue to appear on every published list of growth careers for the future, college students considering career selection consistently overlook the retail sector. Business majors may find their department offers a single course in retailing, but more than likely, retailing is discussed as part of the larger subject area of marketing or consumer behavior.

If retailing is so big now and continues to grow, why aren't business majors more exposed to it in college? One possible reason is that retailing is so varied and so dynamic that it presents real challenges to design one course, much less one chapter of a book, to do justice to such a broad topic. In retailing people can work almost anywhere in the world, with any type of merchandise, for nearly anyone, including themselves. They can work with large corporations or they can work for any of hundreds of thousands of small merchants. Some people forge lasting and rewarding careers in local stores. Others learn the business within one organization and then branch out in business for themselves. The organizational structure of retailing, however, is such that even within a large corporate retailer, being your own boss and independently responsible for your unit is the way business is done.

Furthermore, many, many people are involved in the movement of goods from manufacturer to consumer, and the retail industry hires people with a wide range of talent, from shipping clerks to window designers. We opened this chapter with a definition of the retail industry—that sector of our economy that brings the consumer into direct contact with goods and services. The focus of this career path chapter, and the primary interest of most college graduates, is in the merchandising jobs—buyer, merchandise manager, and store manager.

Focus on Merchandising

Retailing is a term we are all familiar with. We use the term every day to describe the industry that sells us things. Retailing as a technical term, however, most accurately describes the movement of goods from their final point of presentation in the channel of distribution (the retail outlet) to the purchase by the consumer. *Merchandising* is a term used to describe all the buying and selling activities within a store or chain. Merchandise managers decide what to buy based on what will sell. These are immensely complicated decisions.

For example, suppose you are a buyer for men's shirts for a large chain. You must, months in advance of the selling season, choose from among hundreds of fabric possibilities (all cotton, nylon, silk, and blends), weaves (oxford, cambric, poplin, broadcloth, point-on-point, twill), collar styles (button down, tab, many varieties of spread collar, and collarless), cuff styles (French, buttoned), and, of course, price points at which all these various shirt models will be sold. You make all these decisions, including final price, based on a thorough understanding of your market: the people who shop in your store and what they will buy.

This is one of the great areas of confusion about the area of retail merchandising. Many people feel suited to retail because they have "great taste" or "they love to shop." These reasons are not sufficient to get you hired in retail. People who succeed and rise to the top in retail are people who have the best sense of what their market will buy. They develop this strong sensitivity by mixing with the market on the floor. A good merchandiser stays in touch with the customers by working the floor, selling merchandise, hearing complaints and praise about the products, and watching and noting the gender, age, and preferences of the buying public.

It is these positions for which employers are most interested in the talents of the college business major. You've noticed how retailing examples are used over and over again in business texts to illustrate investment principles, risk management, the costs of carrying inventory, pricing strategies, and many other basic principles of sound business management. There's ample evidence that retailing is an important business activity, and yet many business majors don't know very much about it as a career choice. Why is that?

Three Reasons Business Students Don't Consider Retail

There are three principal reasons why business students don't have the opportunity to seriously consider retail careers upon graduation. First and foremost is that the subject of retailing is an art and science unto itself. It is serious big business that incorporates healthy doses of psychology, human behavior, and intuition along with a high tolerance for taking risks. Though there are programs such as the Center for Retailing Studies at Texas A&M where retailing gets the attention it deserves, many business programs simply don't have the faculty expertise to do justice to the exciting, complex, frustrating, and constantly changing field of retail.

The second obvious reason many students fail to consider retail is that retail puts no special premium on the attainment of a college degree. Of course, if you entered the executive suite of our largest retailers, everyone you'd meet would have a college degree. So would most of the preeminent retail managers, sales managers, and buyers. But the emphasis in retail hiring is on decision making, leadership, previous retail exposure, and the ability to juggle an ever-changing workload in a fast-paced environment. In retailing, what you can do and who you are counts more than degree attainment. The following ad for a major national retail chain store manager makes this point—who says you can't have it all?

Store Management: An interesting career . . . a welcome challenge . . . AND rewards. If you're ambitious and determined to make the most of your career, we want you to play an active role in our success and yours! As the nation's leading specialty retailer of imported home furnishings and related items, our store managers are involved in all aspects of our business. That's why we provide a comprehensive on-the-job manager development program to prepare you to take charge of a store, including profit and loss, visual merchandising, and people management.

We seek managers with strong retail experience (college degree a plus), proven leadership abilities, a commitment to customer satisfaction, and the drive to handle a diverse workload in a challenging, fast-paced environment. Candidates must be willing to relocate. Investigate a career that offers it all, including competitive compensation and benefits, and stock purchase/401(k) plans.

The third reason students don't take a more serious look at retailing as they graduate has to do with a misperception of retailing in the hierarchy of American jobs. Let's take a look at a typical college job fair. Business majors are going to be attracted to the professional sales, the large corporations, and the prestige and esteem of classic "management" positions. The retailers may also be at this job fair, but since students haven't had any in-depth exposure to retail careers in their major, all they're apt to see is store management and sales associate jobs. They don't consider the potential here.

The plain and simple reality is that almost any of the retailers present at that job fair will offer careers with more latitude, more fiscal responsibility, more decision-making authority, and more downright opportunities to take off (or crash and burn) than any of the narrowly defined, terminal-in-a-cubicle positions that exist beyond the impressive facades of the corporate management positions. Retailing is about giving talented people an opportunity to chart their own course, within the retailer's concept, for as long as any particular concept remains profitable. Retailers listen to employees' reasoning and, if they find it sound, will support their decisions to add product lines, expand selling space, branch out into new markets, or redefine their image.

Definition of the Career Path

One of the most disappointing realities of any new job for the college graduate is how mundane the first year of employment can be. Students return to visit me and recall how surprised and disheartened they were to find themselves in a supposedly great corporate job, on the management fast track, and yet chained to a desk with very routine, ordinary assignments while they learned the ropes. None of this is true for retailing.

This is the field where you can jump right in and start a career if you are people-oriented, service-oriented, and willing to take advantage of opportunities. Retail personnel are in the front lines of getting the product to the consumer. They are the final marketing intermediaries. Customer contact and customer service are the keys to unlocking the consumer's interest in purchasing your product. Customer contact provides the answers to ordering and pricing mysteries. Customer service is an art and a science, made up of both analytical and communications skills. It is these distinctions that keep your customers coming back.

The four most common entries into retailing for a college graduate are buyer, sales management, store management, and formal retail executive training programs. We will examine each of them in turn.

Buyer/Merchandising Trainee

Buying is the so-called "glamour job" in retailing. Buyers are those individuals whose job it is to choose merchandise. Many people assume buyers are charging all over the globe in search of the most exotic chessboard, or perfect sweaters or inexpensive furniture. But that's hardly the reality.

Most buyers actually spend only a small percentage of their working year in the buying process. And, yes, for some shoes or leather articles, that buying might take place in Italy, but more than likely, most buying will occur at a buying exposition for small leather goods in a convention hall in Atlanta or Dallas.

As a trained buyer, you'll work under the supervision of a senior buyer. You'll need to learn to anticipate your customers' shopping needs several seasons before the merchandise is in the store. You will find yourself considering a variety of issues. Will men switch to a two-button suit? Will misses-sized women tolerate a shorter skirt length? How many of each size children's shoe should you order? And so on. There are mountains of paperwork and sometimes daily reports of sales to analyze. And if you haven't bought right, your mistakes stare back at you from store shelves!

You'll learn to negotiate with vendors on costs, delivery dates, and shared advertising budgets. You will work with store staff on merchandise displays, and as you gain experience, you will take on more responsibility in each of these areas. Before too long, you will be in charge while your senior buyer is away. Some organizations will require that your training include a stint in store management, so you may spend some time in a branch store. Promotion to buyer positions can take two to five years, although movement to middle management is faster than in many other industries.

Sales Management Trainees

We have mentioned the art and science of retail. Sales management is an area where both are especially important. Sales management is the crucial job of providing everything necessary to sell the merchandise you have on the floor. The basic tools in your power kit are sales staff, maintenance of stock, displays, in-store promotional material, and the ambiance you can create with music and lighting.

Your career will begin under a sales department manager whose main responsibilities are the supervision of the sales staff, the productivity and profitability of the department, and the physical configuration, including displays, signage, and racks within the department. Sales managers and their assistants work closely with buyers and their duties sometimes overlap, especially in the areas of inventory control and turnover of merchandise.

You'll be learning the merchandise, working the floor, scheduling staff, arranging displays, anything and everything to keep your department running smoothly. This is a hands-on, roll-up-your-sleeves, dig in and get involved kind of job.

Typical paths are trainee, assistant department manager, department manager, assistant store manager, store manager, and on to vice president. There is considerable movement of sales management staff from store to store, and relocation as part of a promotion is common for successful managers. Workloads may be heavy, but rewards of rapid advancement are there.

Store Management

The goal of the store manager, in any size operation, is to run the store at a profit. Store management involves the merchandising functions discussed above, with the addition of store operations (staffing, shipping, receiving), accounting, and advertising. In smaller stores or decentralized branches of larger chains, the store manager might handle all of these functions. The central office, however, often provides varying degrees of assistance with advertising layout, administrative forms, policy statements, and training. In a larger store, the store manager would have assistant managers handling each of these functions. Chain stores with centralized administrative functions would control all accounting and buying and probably supply all advertising setups, relieving individual store management of those functions.

Executive Training Programs

Your entry title in either of the general paths listed above would be termed a "trainee" position, and that is not just to emphasize that they are entry-level. Most retailers have developed very sophisticated and comprehensive executive training programs in both the sales management and buyer categories that allow trainees to move through a number of carefully designed training seminars and related work assignments. Excellent classroom presentations by senior executives combined with practical, hands-on experience are a highly effective way to learn your job and, more important, to succeed in it!

Working Conditions

This work is fast paced, at times exciting, with numerous opportunities to connect with the public and respond to its needs. Retailing is a career that rewards your ability to sense and stay ahead of consumers' wants and needs. There are drawbacks, however, as with any job. Retailing often involves long hours and, at the beginning of your career, a not-very-exciting paycheck as well as some very mundane chores.

Be ready to accept some drudgery in your job. You'll need reserves of physical stamina. Even senior managers, on occasions, have to plunge in and help shift stock, relocate racks, or change displays. In retailing there are no primo dons or prima donnas. Everyone pitches in and does what is necessary to move merchandise.

In addition to physical stamina, you'll have to be willing to tolerate risk. Retailing means playing the roulette wheel of trying to anticipate what the market will want six or nine months in the future—ordering all that merchandise in the size, colors, and quantities now for a future you can't entirely predict.

Everyone in this industry will agree on one thing: for those who love it, if you demonstrate your zeal and enthusiasm with competency, you can expect to be recognized early on and rewarded with promotions and bigger paychecks.

Job factors given below are among the most important when making a considered choice to pursue retailing as a career. As you read these, compare these jobs demands to the results of the self-assessment you did after reading Chapter 1 of this book.

Rapid Advancement

Ambitious people usually want positions that demonstrate their talent to advantage and then reward that talent with responsibilities and duties that will further stretch and develop their skills. Retailing offers these possibilities. Talent is immediately recognizable in the fast-paced and highly responsive world of retailing.

Suppose one of your first assignments as a buyer trainee is to purchase the comforters for the bedding department—hundreds of thousands of dollars worth of decisions involving fabric composition, stuffing contents, price range, crucial color and design choices, and, of course, various price lines and sizes. If you choose well, your stock moves off the shelf and daily sales reports trumpet your success to store executives. If not, you see your mistakes every time you visit the floor.

Action

Some people love to be busy, the busier the better. They cannot tolerate sitting at a desk all day, chatting around the water fountain, or catching up on business journals. They seek action and avoid the boring and repetitive. The answer is retailing. No day is like another, and the only constant is change. Each day has a different outcome as each customer through the door presents a different collection of needs to be satisfied. Merchandise arrives daily, customers need to be serviced, stock must be rearranged or freshened, and paperwork demands attention. Demands can be incessant. This is a business for the strong and energetic. The pace is fast, exciting, and fulfilling, but only if you enjoy the work. If you're not happy, you'll see it as chaotic, frantic, and frustrating!

Contact with People

Sometimes job applicants make the mistake of telling the interviewer "I'm a people person." What does that really mean? In retailing, a "people person" must be comfortable with all kinds of people from all walks of life and, increasingly, from many different parts of the world. You will have to want to understand their needs and enjoy making an effort to fulfill those needs.

Merchandise

To be the most effective you can be in retailing, you need to enjoy and appreciate what you sell. If you don't, how you display it, how you talk about it, and how you feature it in your store will betray your lack of interest. Retailing is about the goods that are sold, and there should be an enthusiasm on your part for that merchandise, whether it's snowblowers or fine bed linens. Retailers who love their merchandise convey that enthusiasm to their markets.

Mobility

Retailing careers offer unparalleled mobility. Retail opportunities exist worldwide and in every size and variety of emporium, so if you are anxious to live on the West Coast or in the Plains states, you can do it.

Entrepreneurship

The word *entrepreneurship* has special meaning for retailers because, in a sense, every buyer, merchandise manager, or store owner is in business for him- or herself. Retail structure encourages you to think for yourself, make decisions, and run your operation as if it were your own business. Each department or operating unit in today's retail stores has its own printout of profit and loss. You will easily be able to demonstrate your entrepreneurial spirit.

But working within the retail establishment is also the best preparation for a career as an independent retailer. As a buyer, merchandise manager, or store manager, you'll be exposed to many of the issues, concerns, and decisions that you would have to make if you were running your own business.

Travel

If you're an auditor in the accounting industry, you expect to travel to clients and may stay for a week at a time. Sales representatives frequently travel and stay overnight. Retail positions, however, have very little associated travel, although most retailers get welcomed opportunities, on occasion, to travel to a trade show or product fair. Top buyers for large stores often travel to locate goods to sell, and some buyers travel to foreign markets frequently, but buying trips tend to be limited in time and restricted to particular times of the year.

Work

Everybody works, and there's no place to hide. The work may not be arduous, but it never ends. Everyone is expected to pitch in when needed, and those who don't are easily noticed.

Long Hours

Take a look around. Retailers are open holidays (even some of the most sacrosanct, such as Christmas), evenings, weekends, and late nights. Stores need to be staffed and maintained and managed. You'll be working many times when the rest of the world is out playing! Retailers soon learn that they work when others play or have holidays, and they have time off when everyone seems to be at work! Competition is intense in retail, and management often puts in long hours on and off the floor to stay abreast of the competition.

No Glamour

Even when you obtain the coveted position of buyer, you'll be shocked to find your office is a cubbyhole tucked behind the dressing rooms on the fifth floor. Store floor space is for merchandise. Employees take what's not usable or left over. A very successful buyer for leather goods for a famous New York store once told my students, "If you think visiting Florence, Italy, is glamorous, you ought to see me in July on the bed in my hotel room eating a tuna-fish sandwich and trying to decide how many of which gloves I should order for next winter!" Is that glamorous? I don't think so. Glamour is for the customers.

Training and Qualifications

The environment of retailing is less one of glamour, travel, and clothes than one of computer printouts and statements of profit and loss. You need to have an entrepreneurial spirit of excitement about running your own million-dollar department and making solid, increasing profits because those are the factors that move retailers ahead. Of course, retailing has many attractive, exciting, and, yes, even some glamorous aspects, but to base your career decision on those expectations is to invite disappointment by misunderstanding the basic concepts of the retail trade.

Because computerized information can tell the retailer so much about what is required in terms of inventory, labor, and so on, students seriously considering retail careers need to consider mastering computer technology, including spreadsheet software and statistical packages, and have some exposure to database management. As our economy becomes increasingly technologically oriented, the candidate who can apply high-tech, information-based skills to a successful career in retailing has many advantages.

In addition to these technical skills, there is a need for analytical skills. Accounting and business organization courses give you the solid basic background you'll need to understand the language and culture of a business climate. Courses in marketing, general management, and economics will give you an even broader picture of the changing and very dynamic scope of retailing in our economy. The appearance of increasingly large merchandisers, whether they are department stores, warehouse showrooms, or grocery retailers, places demands on those candidates to understand the mechanics of "big" business.

Join marketing or retail clubs, if your college offers them, and participate actively. These groups may provide an opportunity to work with retail people outside of the college environment. That will help in your future dealings with people from a variety of backgrounds.

Internships or a co-op program, if your school has one, are ideal ways to help you ascertain your interest and suitability for the retail profession. Additionally, they help you to add valuable entries on your résumé that will attract employers following graduation.

Part-time employment in any area of the retail sector will give you immense credibility as a manager who can truthfully say to rank-and-file workers, "I've done that."

Retailing is about people, not just machines, and it is this combination of the technological and human that demands the retailing candidate have some exposure to other cultures, anthropology, sociology, and psychology. This background will help in understanding your market, communicating with its members, and assessing their needs and wants.

Earnings

The most recent salary survey conducted by the College Placement Council (now called the National Association of Colleges and Employers) shows starting salaries increasing modestly at this point for general undergraduate business majors entering retailing, though increasing somewhat more strongly for those business students who have elected a retailing or merchandise management major. Earnings vary according to the size of the retail establishment. But remember: retailing is one of the few sectors of employment where there is a direct compensation for the volume and quality of the work accomplished. Thus, even without a graduate degree, you have opportunities to boost your pay through outstanding performance. The *Boston Globe*, in an article on job outlooks for 1995 graduates, quoted the Collegiate Employment Research Institute at Michigan State University as estimating starting salaries for college graduates with business majors entering retailing at $22,195, a 1.6 percent increase over 1993–94 salaries. In 2002, retail sales managers and first-line sales supervisors were making a median salary of $27,510 nationwide, government figures showed. The following are some very general guidelines.

General merchandise managers (GMM) usually have vice president status and overall responsibility for a major division of a store. While not involved in actual buying, they coordinate buying and selling activities for departments within their divisions. They also plan sales promotions, determine quantity of merchandise to be stocked, and decide markups and markdowns. These positions report directly to the chief executive officer.

Divisional merchandise managers (DMM) report to the GMM and are responsible for one (or more) of the classifications of merchandise within the division. So, in a home supply store, it might be garden equipment, furniture, and lighting. In a department store, it might be juniors coats, dresses, and sportswear. The DMM's first duty is to achieve the profit and sales goals set for the department by top management. With the help of the buyers under his or her supervision, the DMM keeps stock of merchandise, displays, replenishment, and sales movement.

Both GMMs and DMMs are college graduates in the large retail corporations of today and many have achieved these positions following years of floor work, stints as buyers, and the usual path of advancement to top management. Salaries vary widely and according to size of employer, volume of sales, and potential for bonus. Salary ranges for these positions are as follows:

General merchandise manager $60,000 to $200,000
Divisional merchandise manager $50,000 to $120,000

Buyers seek out and purchase all the items stocked by a retail store, from can openers to diamonds. The argument over the degree of glamour in these jobs will never cease. Nevertheless, these positions do involve some travel and occasionally (depending upon the store and what is being purchased) foreign travel. Using past experience or market research as a guide they buy what they believe will sell in their stores. About 140,000 buyers work in retail stores around the country, and most are located in major metropolitan areas. Generally, these positions require the breadth and quantitative exposure of a college degree, although the training comes from the store where they begin as assistant buyers or buyer trainees. Earnings vary as discussed, and the median in 2001 was $37,000-plus; but those at the top end of the buyers category make $40,000 to $80,000. The low end starts at about $22,000.

Assistant buyers or buyer trainees are in training to become buyers. While training is under way (at least twelve months to follow the yearly cycle), assistant buyers manage voluminous paperwork, process orders from vendors, check invoices on material received, and keep track of stock. The salary range for junior to senior assistant buyers is $20,000 to $50,000 depending upon store size, volume of traffic, and so on.

Department managers oversee the selling floor and stock areas. They ensure merchandise is properly ticketed, markdowns are taken, displays are well stocked, the selling area is in order, and sales staff coverage is adequate. Earnings range between $15,000 to $50,000.

Sales staff number over three million people employed in retail businesses altogether, with the largest numbers of sales staff in department stores. Solid training programs often begin sales staff in areas requiring little customer assistance (housewares, notions, etc.) and build experience to those departments with "big ticket" and greater customer assistance, such as in furniture, designer labels, custom tailoring, or appliances. Salaries vary dramatically from hourly wages of minimum wage to as much as $50,000 a year.

Career Outlook

According to the U.S. Department of Labor's Bureau of Labor Statistics, as many as 510,000 new jobs in retail sales may be created through the year 2010.

Consolidation of buying activities because of mergers among organizations will reduce the demand for buyers through the year 2010, except in farm products sales. Although the same industry conditions exist for sales managers, the number of store outlets will keep this job category growing at an average rate.

The variety and scope of retailing today is obvious to us all. Disposable income is increasing among the middle and upper-middle classes and people are constantly seeking retail outlets that offer the mix of goods they want.

As the largest segment of our population—the "baby boomers"—reaches their peak earning years, demographics suggest an increasing demand for retailing services and the management staff to direct those services.

Strategy for Finding the Jobs

Retailing holds many exciting possibilities for the business graduate. The jobs are creative, demanding, and well worth your investment in a college education. The future of retailing is full of surprises but is certain to include increased technology and innovative new ways to both reach and satisfy the consumer market.

The statistics given on earnings certainly make the profession a desirable one. And the projections of growth in the retail sector should lead you to the conviction that if you really want to enter retailing as a career and have the personal characteristics the industry is seeking, there is a job waiting for you.

Retailing is, however, an incredibly diverse field. Merchandise lines run the gamut from lingerie to lawnmowers, and there are big names in each field (Victoria's Secret/John Deere). Geographically, retailing is literally "all over the map," and you can find retail employment throughout the United States and the world. Once you're located somewhere, there is equally as much choice about job duties: buyer, merchandise manager, store or department manager, site development, advertising, finance—the list goes on and on.

With the following outline you can develop a successful strategy for finding the right job for you in the retail sector. If you (1) have enough time to do a thorough job search, (2) have access to all the options listed below, and (3) want to be sure you've covered all possibilities, then go through this plan step by step. Not only will you succeed in finding the jobs, but the process of implementing this search will also make you a better and more informed interview candidate and increase your chances of being selected because you will truly understand the world of retail. However, if time or your options are limited, then pick and choose among this list for what is most doable for you.

Essential Preparation

If you're a business major, your own school is apt to have plenty of ways for you to get your career search in high gear, and you should be sure to take advantage of them. Some of these may include:

Marketing/Retail Clubs. Business clubs that bring majors together for common interests are wonderful sources of information about a possible career in retailing. Try to meet the guest speakers who come to campus to speak to the club on business issues. Let them know of your career plans and ask their advice. Serve on speaker committees and special career-related projects. If your club has an opportunity to attend a national convention, try to be part of your school team and use that opportunity to meet guests, gather information, and network.

Cooperative Education. Your college may provide an opportunity for you to elect a work/study plan called co-op. If you can manage it (it may add anywhere from a semester to a full year to your degree), cooperative education is a proven way to access a career, learn the ropes, meet influential people in your field, and be exposed to the dimensions of your chosen career area while you earn some money for tuition.

Internships. The single most effective way to improve your ability to move from graduation to a job is through an internship. Internships are generally nonpaid or low-paid training positions in your chosen field that give you broad exposure to a variety of tasks and management role models. They can last from a few weeks to a semester and sometimes longer. Internships can often be used for college credit toward your degree. Many successful interns have been offered positions at their internship sponsoring organization upon graduation. Many more credit their job success to their internship. *Internships 2003*, a Peterson publication, lists some superb retail internship opportunities.

Alumni Career Connections. Either the career office or alumni office on your campus can put you in touch with former graduates of your college who are now working in the retail job market. These alumni connections can be very helpful, offering informational interviews, background on the firms that employ them, and general insights into the retail job market. Depending upon the sophistication of your school's alumni database, it may be possible to identify who's working as a buyer, a merchandiser, or a store manager. Remember, when contacting these individuals for career guidance, that you are representing your college and every other student who may someday want to use this valuable referral service. Be prepared with a list of questions for your alumni contact and use his or her time wisely. You'll make a good friend and have increased insight into your chosen career field. Many alumni will invite you (distances permitting) for a visit to their place of business and may offer to assist with your résumé or job search strategy.

Campus Job Postings. The binders that contain some of the hundreds of job advertisements that come through the mail to your career office on campus can inform you of many excellent retail entry-level jobs. These may be duplications of the advertising copy that was placed into a newspaper classified want-ad section, or it may be a special recruitment mailing to a local college for qualified applicants. These job postings are easy to flip through and, because they change frequently (new ones arrive weekly), you should make this kind of "catalog shopping" a weekly activity!

On-Campus Recruiting. The employers from the retail sector who visit your campus are giving you a strong indication of their interest in your school's students. Sign up for every recruitment interview with a retailer that you possibly can. On-campus interviewing can and does lead to job offers. It's excellent interview practice, as well. Most important, you will begin to develop a sense of what each employer is offering and start to make distinctions about what you feel is the best "fit" for you in a retail career offering. Unlike the job fairs, these are private interviews, one-on-one with a senior representative from the retail organization. Even better, it's held on campus in familiar surroundings, which should prove helpful to you in controlling those interview jitters. Your campus career office probably maintains files on all the recruiting firms to allow you to be thoroughly prepared for your interview.

Job Fairs. Job fairs are valuable job search tools for the student seeking a retail career opening. First, they are very efficient. How else would you be able to meet and talk with so many possible job contacts in one day? Second, retailers use them! Rosters of employers at past job fairs indicate retailers are traditionally very well represented. Retailers enjoy participating in job fairs because it allows them to meet and see a number of highly qualified business majors. Third, the job fair process of walking up to an employment representative, greeting him or her, and giving a one-minute "infomercial" about who you are and what you might have to offer the organization is a perfect example of the specific kind of people skills retailers seek out.

If a recruiter at a job fair is interested in you, he or she may ask you to submit a formal application or invite you to one of the employer's open houses or an actual interview. The recruiter may extend this invitation at the job fair or by telephone or letter at a later date. Strong student job candidates who take full advantage of job fair opportunities are consistently amazed at both the number of responses and how much later after the fair some of them arrive.

"Careers 2003," the nation's number one college recruitment conference (careerconferences.com), always offers a premier gathering of some of the country's top retailers at its annual job fairs for college seniors each spring in Puerto Rico, New York, Atlanta, Washington, D.C., and Chicago. Your career office at college will have application forms for this prescreened job fair as well as a folder of other forthcoming job fairs in your area that will be featuring jobs in retail. Some of these fairs are free; some have a modest fee. Take advantage of all of them to vastly improve the efficiency of your job search.

The Classic Cover Letter/Résumé Campaign

Get to your nearest college library and dig out some of the excellent reference books listed in the bibliography at the back of this book. Books such as *The 100 Best Companies to Work for in America* or *The Encyclopedia of Business Information Sources* (see Additional Resources section) might be a good beginning. Start to list all of the retailers you might enjoy working for and send them your résumé with an interesting, informative cover letter. Be ready to follow up your letter with a phone call and see if you can arrange an interview. Don't be concerned if the retailer's headquarters are far away from your campus. The retailer may have an executive attending a conference in a nearby city who could interview you, or a senior buyer at a trade show might have time to meet and talk with you and report back to the home office about the impression you made.

The Option of "Temping"

The benefits of temping are significant and the benefits to the employer are well known: no cost for providing employee benefits, no commitment, and the ability to expand or shrink the workforce according to demand without severance costs or legal problems.

For you, the advantages are a chance to look inside the kind of organization you might eventually call home. You'll be paid for your work, of course, but more important, you'll meet people, network, add a relevant job to your résumé, and perhaps be able to access the organization's internal posting system. Temping has changed. Once a source of clerical and light industrial workers, now temping provides any level of professional or managerial expertise needed.

Some Special Interview Tips for Talking with Retailers

Eventually you are going to be called upon to sit down and interview for your position. While this book contains some valuable advice for excelling during an interview, polish and high performance will come with experience. That said, there are three special considerations you'll want to be aware of in talking to professionals in the world of retail:

1. Be prepared to talk trends! Each issue of the major business magazines has information on retailing or selling, or economic data tracking current trends in population, changing lifestyles, and buying patterns that form the seeds of present and emerging strategies and technologies for selling in the retail sector.

2. Understand consumer behavior. Your business curriculum probably included some marketing courses, including consumer behavior. Just as important are courses in the liberal arts, such as psychology, sociology, anthropology, and philosophy. They help you as a potential retail employee to understand better and, consequently, interact more effectively with the consumer.

3. Are you ready to analyze? Good retailers take accounting and business organization courses to learn the language and understand the structure of business. Jobs in retailing center around analysis but require superb "people" skills as well.

Possible Employers

Any retailer would be pleased to add to its employment ranks a freshly minted college graduate interested in a career in merchandising. That doesn't mean, however, that you should be interested in just any retailer! This book has made a strong case for using your employment to add portable skills to your résumé—skills that are not industry specific but that you can take with you from job to job. One of the best ways to ensure you are adding those skills is by selecting employment sites with high-quality management, a respect for college education, and training options. The following retailers provide these:

Bob's Stores
Attn: Bruce Wallace, Recruiter
160 Corporate Ct.
Meriden, CT 06450
bobstores.com

Bob's is the original casual clothing and footwear superstore and a subsidiary of Melville Corporation, the parent company of CVS, Marshalls, Thom McAn, Linens 'n Things, and other successful businesses. Bob's recruits management trainees for additional new stores. The company is primarily interested in business, management, and marketing majors. Management trainees take part in a twelve-week training program that rotates through all areas of the stores.

JC Penney Company, Inc.
Attn: Michael Silipo, College Relations Manager
6501 Legacy Dr.
Plano, TX 75024
jcpenney.com
JC Penney is one of the nation's top retailers and enjoys a leadership position in the fashion industry. JC Penney hires more college graduates than any other retailer.

Office Depot, Inc.
College Relations
2200 Old Germantown Rd.
Delray Beach, FL 33445
officedepot.com
The number one retail office-products company with more than four hundred stores in the United States and Canada, Office Depot offers formal management training, ongoing leadership skills development, a superb benefits package, and excellent advancement opportunities.

Saks Fifth Avenue
Manager of College Relations
Saks Inc.
750 Lakeshore Pkwy.
Birmingham, AL 35211
saksincorporated.com
Currently operating in forty-five locations across the nation with sales of more than $1 billion annually, Saks is committed to training top buyers and managers through its Executive Training Program, based in New York. Two distinct paths are available in the buyer program (store management path or merchandise management path), both offering comprehensive training and eligibility for an assistant buyer position. Saks Inc. also operates the Carson's, Herbergers, and Younkers chains, among others.

Sears Roebuck & Co.
College Relations Team
3333 Beverly Rd., Location D4-171D
Hoffman Estates, IL 60179
sears.com/collegerecruit
Sears has a long history as a successful and innovative retailer. It is one of the largest retailers in the world, based on merchandise sales and service, employing more than 350,000 associates. Among its strengths are a loyal customer base, a powerful network of retail stores, highly focused product lines, national service and delivery organizations, and credit operations. Sears provides a challenging work environment and recognizes individual and team contributions.

Talbots, Human Resources
Attn: Terri Smalley
175 Beal St.
Hingham, MA 02043
talbots.com
An upscale women's chain of more than 350 stores, Talbots values individual challenge, ability, and effort with programs in finance, marketing, merchandising, and advertising/catalog in a fast-paced retail environment.

Toys "R" Us or Kids "R" Us
Human Resources
461 From Rd.
Paramus, NJ 07652
toysrus.com
These two stores (which hire separately, so send separate résumés to each store's human resource staff) have made children's toys and fashion a $9 billion dollar business with more than 40,000 employees. They value fast learners and creative thinkers who are still kids at heart and see life as a world of possibilities.

Wal-Mart Stores, Inc.
Attn: Brenda A. Domingues, College Coordinator
Bentonville, AR 72716-8611
(877) 583-1343 (toll-free)
Fax: (479) 277-1013
crwebq@Wal-Mart.com

The first Wal-Mart opened in 1962 (in Rogers, Arkansas), and the rest is retailing history—Wal-Mart is one of the largest companies in the world. Sales for fiscal 2002 were $217 billion from Wal-Mart stores, Supercenters, Sam's Clubs, and neighborhood markets. College graduates are needed for the assistant manager trainee program.

Possible Job Titles

Assistant buyer	Merchandise manager
Buyer	Sales associate
Buyer trainee	Store manager
Department manager	

Related Occupations

Comparison shopper	Retail sales workers
Insurance agent	Services sales representative
Manufacturer's representatives	Traffic managers
Procurement services managers	Wholesale sales representative

Professional Associations

American Marketing Association
250 S. Wacker Dr., Suite 5800
Chicago, IL 60606
(312) 542-9000
marketingpower.org
Members/Purpose: Professional society of marketing and marketing research executives, sales and promotion managers, advertising specialists, and others interested in marketing.
Publications: *American Marketing Association—Proceedings*, *International Membership Directory*, *Journal of Health Care Marketing*.

American Money Management Association
2135 Bering Dr.
Houston, TX 77057-3711
Members/Purpose: Corporations, credit unions, associations, savings and
loans, and banks. Provides money management, financial planning, and
insurance services.

ARMS—The Association of Retail
  Marketing Services
244 Broad St.
Red Bank, NJ 07701
(732) 842-5070
Members/Purpose: Devoted to the promotional needs of the retail
industry. Recommends incentive promotion at the retail level.
Publications: *ARMS—Membership Directory, Directory of Top 50 Wholesale
Grocers, Top 100 Grocery Chains.*

Food Business Forum
8445 Colesville Rd., Suite 710
Silver Spring, MD 20910
ciesnet.com
Members/Purpose: Fosters cooperation between chain store organizations
and the suppliers. Serves as liaison between members. Assists in the
exchange of trainees among member firms.
Publications: *Euro Food Focus*, membership directory.

Institute of
  Store Planners
25 N. Broadway
Tarrytown, NY 10591
(914) 332-1806
ispo.org
Members/Purpose: Persons active in store planning and design, visual
merchandisers, students and educators, contractors and suppliers to the
industry. Dedicated to the professional growth of members while
providing service to the public through improvement of the retail
environment.
Publications: *Directory of Store Planners and Consultants, ISP International
News*, newsletter.

International Mass Retail Association (IMRA)
1700 N. Moore St., Suite 2250
Arlington, VA 22209
(703) 841-2300
imra.org
Members/Purpose: Purpose is to conduct research and educational programs on every phase of self-service general merchandising retailing.
Training: Conduct seminars and workshops.
Publications: *IMRA Membership Directory and Exposition Guide, Operating Results of Mass Retail Stores, Perquisites in Mass Retailing, Shrinkage Study, State Legislative Service.*

Museum Store Association
4100 E. Mississippi Ave., Suite 800
Denver, CO 80246-3055
(303) 504-9223
msaweb.org
Members/Purpose: Sales departments in museums, including museums of fine arts, history, ethnology, and science. Encourages dialogue and assistance among members.
Publications: membership list, *Museum Store, Product News.*

National Association of
  Men's Sportswear Buyers
309 Fifth Ave., Suite 303
New York, NY 10016
(212) 685-4550
namsbworldsource.com, nsi-shows.com
Members/Purpose: Sponsors trade shows for buyers of clothes for menswear stores. Conducts media interviews to discuss menswear and educational programs. Sponsors NAMSB WorldSource show for U.S. buyers to meet with global sourcing contacts.
Publications: Newsletter, also distributes fashion videotapes.

National Retail Federation (NRF)
325 Seventh St. NW, Suite 1100
Washington, DC 20004
(202) 783-7971
nrf.com

Members/Purpose: Department, chain, mass merchandise, and specialty stores retailing men's, women's, and children's apparel and home furnishings.

Training: Conducts conferences and workshops. Provides recruitment and training.

Publications: *Retail Control, STORES* magazine.

Office Products Representatives Alliance
Business Products Industry Association
301 N. Fairfax St.
Alexandria, VA 22314
(703) 549-9040
bpia.org

Members/Purpose: Objectives are to serve as a resource for branch store dealers, to help increase professionalism, and to develop ways to combat competition. Seeks to explore areas of interest for retail dealers, including merchandising and product representation, advertising, store financing, personnel development and training, and strategic business planning.

Publication: *Dealer Operating Profile.*

Retail Advertising and Marketing Association, International (RAMA)
333 N. Michigan Ave., Suite 3000
Chicago, IL 60601
(312) 251-7262
ramarac.org

Members/Purpose: Persons in retail sales promotion and advertising and persons serving retailers in promotional capacities.

Publications: *RAC Digest, Who's Who in Retail Advertising.*

8

Path 3: Health Care

One of the first hints that the health-care field may prove agreeable to you as a new business graduate is the terminology currently of importance in this field: physician's corporation, managed care, health maintenance organization. Health care is big business, no question. More significant, however, is the fact that it is a business that is under heavy scrutiny to do a good job. The government watches health care, physicians have a vested interest, vendors and suppliers have every reason to pay careful attention, and the public, most of all, pays close attention to even the smallest change in health-care provisions.

Why? The reasons are largely economic in every instance. Health-care costs are steadily increasing, and as those costs increase, the employers and individuals who pay for health care complain. Here's an example. We are all quite familiar with natural childbirthing techniques. Natural childbirth is best defined as childbirth with prepared parents who have received education about the birthing process and who hope to experience the birth with a minimum of anesthetics or other drugs. (Having fewer drugs makes for a healthier baby and a faster recovery for the mother.)

Years ago, women stayed in the hospital for lengthy confinements. They delivered their babies under heavier anesthetics, which required more recuperation time. They also stayed in the hospital to learn about baby care from medical professionals. At that time, hospital costs were not as dramatic as they are now. But things have changed.

Hospital stays began to shorten considerably. Parents became better educated about child care, mothers were using very little medication, and we realized long hospital stays were increasingly costly and not a good use of medical staff. Others could teach parents about new-baby care more efficiently and more cheaply outside the hospital.

Business Sensitivity to Medical Issues

The controversy in the medical and popular press is that stays for childbirth have shortened too much. Hospital stays have now become as short as two or three days, and many women who have uncomplicated deliveries are being discharged after one night's stay or, in the most extreme cases, after as little as twelve hours! Insurance companies reward brief stays to encourage reduced costs. The U.S. Centers for Disease Control and Prevention reports that hospital stays for vaginal births have dropped from an average of 3.9 days in 1970 to 2.5 in 1999.

When length of stay dropped too low, legislators in Massachusetts, New Jersey, and Maryland actually passed laws regulating hospital stays for childbirth, and Congress later passed a federal law as well. What's going on here?

What's going on is health-care reform, a constant process that sometimes becomes a battle between health-care professionals and cost-containment interests—insurance companies, hospital administrators, employers who provide insurance, and government agencies including Medicaid and Medicare. Health-care professionals want to provide patients with the very best health care they can. Increasingly, the cost of providing that care has escalated as larger and larger monetary judgments are made against health-care providers for mistakes, omissions, or in some cases, malpractice. A significant increase in health-care costs is attributable to the threat of litigation.

Insurers and health-care cost-containment professionals want costs to stay as low as possible, and all have different reasons. Some want to make a profit on their policies; others want low costs to keep care affordable to as much of the public as possible.

This is obviously a situation that cries out for good business skills and management that is sensitive to the public's health-care and financial needs. Doctors and nurses provide quality health care, administrators manage paperwork, and insurers watch bills, but who is looking at the overall system? The important adjuncts of the treatment process are patient screening, long wait lines for services, presence or lack of amenities such as food services, shopping, and convenient parking at health-care providers. How successful can a doctor/patient interaction be if the patient wasn't able to find a parking space or feels the parking fee was too high, or has waited in line for an hour only to be confronted with paperwork he or she cannot understand? Business concepts such as process redesign can help. There's a place for business expertise alongside clinical care within today's health-care delivery networks.

Definition of the Career Path

Health care is changing—fewer jobs are in traditional hospital settings, and more jobs are migrating to other places in the health network, such as out-patient treatment centers, medical office buildings, and skilled-care facilities. Because there are so many available job sites, each with its own unique conditions, let's begin by looking at a number of health-care positions available to a recent graduate with a business degree. A good start might be with a position that emphasizes some of those skills and attributes we associate with the business degree. The following position is located within a major health maintenance organization (HMO) in the greater Boston area:

Assistant Home Care Contract Administrator: Responsibilities include negotiation and administration of contracts for home care services. Under direction of the Administrator, you will develop reimbursement agreements, ensure contract compliance, administer contracts, and perform cost and utilization analysis. Requirements include:

- B.A./B.S. in business or a health-care field
- Proficiency in Lotus 1-2-3/Excel
- Willingness to participate in training/workshops to acquire clinical/ technical background in infusion therapy, DME, and respiratory services.

Here's a marvelous entry-level opportunity that will really groom you in the field of contract administration, specifically in the field of respiratory therapy. It will draw upon your computer skills, your economics classes, your business law course, and many others. This is the kind of exciting position that transforms a generalist business major into a skilled professional.

This next position is also for an HMO, another large and well-known entity with a reputation for excellent management. This position has a quantitative side, too, but with an emphasis on sales and promotion as well.

Account Manager: Oversee the day-to-day operational aspects of medical benefit plan administration for major existing accounts; providing ongoing guidance to major accounts with respect to projecting and planning for future medical benefit needs; working with underwriting, communications, and enrollment departments to initiate and complete annual renewals; and providing education regarding plan guidelines and benefits.

To be considered, you must have a bachelor's degree in business or the equivalent and one to three years of related experience in a sales or service capacity. Strong communication and presentations skills are essential. Knowledge of self-funded and managed-care health benefits preferred. Extensive local travel will be involved.

The following position is more suited to the graduate who enjoyed marketing courses or consumer behavior. This advertisement is for a position in a small to mid-sized hospital:

Manager, Media Relations and Special Events: If you have excellent writing, interviewing, media relations, editing, and supervisory skills this might be the right position for you. Individual will be responsible for project management in media relations and special events as well as developing community outreach programs such as lecture series, public forums, etc. Position requires a bachelor's degree in business, marketing, journalism, health care, or a related field.

Granted, the subject matter of your copywriting may be issues such as how to prevent osteoporosis or common skiing injuries and how to avoid them. The language and level of sophistication is for a general audience, and you will have professionals available to check the accuracy of the text. The craft and technique of media relations and special events remains the same. This is an exciting position on its own, and also one that could propel you to a larger medical facility or health maintenance organization, to magazines or other media specializing in health issues, or into the commercial world.

One item you've probably noticed in these job listings is the requirement for a business degree *or* health-care background. There are a couple of reasons for this lack of insistence on a health-care-specific degree. First, some of these job specialties are relatively new and it would be foolish to demand what the job market cannot provide. Health-care degrees are still in short supply, and many of those graduating from health-care programs are more interested in clinical (patient contact) positions, not administration or management.

The second reason for some equivocation in degree or experience requirements is that the industry itself is not sure which expertise is most critical, the management or the medical! Right now, in similar jobs all over the country, there are professionals from both backgrounds doing excellent work. At the top of the profession are physician executives educated in medicine and business, and paid accordingly, working as hospital system CEOs.

If you're exploring the health-care field as a business graduate, part of that interest may stem from an interest in people and their well-being, so you may want some contact with the patient population. You can have this! Let's look at a couple of recently advertised positions that would offer some of that patient contact. Here's a hospital-based position:

Executive Directors: Will be the senior manager in our adult day-care center and is responsible for all aspects of a center's operation: meeting census and payer mix objectives; providing outcome-based care according to company standards; continuously improving center efficiency and achieving profitability targets. At least 50 percent of the ED's time will be spent on marketing and sales. He or she must have the following qualifications:
- Some previous management experience
- B.A. degree
- Willingness and ability to sell service to community
- High energy, enthusiasm, warmth, and compassion

To do this job well, you'll need to know your market. You'll need to appreciate what motivates individuals to place parents or relatives in adult day care, and you'll want to mix with the clients to learn their stories and their complaints and satisfactions with the care they're receiving. Though the patient population here is, by and large, healthier, you will encounter clients with eating difficulties, hearing loss, poor vision, and perhaps symptoms of presenility, dementia, or early stages of Alzheimer's disease.

Reading these advertisements, you may be interested in the jobs but concerned that you don't understand all the medical jargon and terminology. Actually, even medical professionals struggle with the lingo outside their areas of expertise. You've encountered a number of terms in these ads: *respiratory therapy, continuous quality improvement, census, payer mix, DME, rehabilita-*

tion, and so on. Don't be dismayed. Every field of work has its own vocabulary. The terminology of the stock market is equally confusing to the uninitiated. What do you do?

Consult a dictionary! *Black's Medical Dictionary, Stedman's Medical Dictionary,* or the *Merriam Webster Medical Dictionary* (all listed in Additional Resources and generally available in larger reference libraries) are a few examples of the many resources available to you. Certainly, you'll want to investigate and understand any terminology in the job ad itself and, once on the job, begin a regular self-tutorial to learn the vocabulary of your new environment. If necessary, you can also pursue education—advanced degrees in health administration or public health or a certificate in one of the allied health professions.

How patients enter, are processed, and discharged from a facility is not just a cost issue, but a patient care issue. Repeat business in situations where clients can select their provider may be in large part influenced by how smoothly they felt the administrative process was managed. On the patient care side, an agitated, anxious patient who has been waiting too long, is overly confused by paperwork, or whose admission records are missing is harder to treat and takes longer to respond to treatment. The individual whose job is to facilitate the administrative process can have a positive and direct effect on a patient's well-being.

Working Conditions

We've looked at a variety of job types and environments. Despite the variety, however, there are still some generalizations we can make about working conditions that can guide you in your job search.

Behind the Scenes

The administrative, quantitative, computer-oriented, and analysis jobs are going to be located, in most cases, in the offices and administrative suites that lie behind the scenes of patient care. While some of these kinds of offices may be located in a section of a health-care facility, many are not; they are situated in office buildings indistinguishable from neighboring buildings. Billing services for a radiological corporation of physicians may not even be located in the same town as the medical office. So even though you are in health care, you are not necessarily at a work site where health care is being delivered. That may or may not be your preference.

On the Front Lines

There are, however, numerous jobs sited at hospitals, adult day-care facilities, nursing homes, rehabilitation centers, health maintenance clinics, and other locations that receive a constant flow of patients and their families. In some of the jobs we have listed, some contact with the patients is important to do the best job possible. If you're a patient care administrator, not only will you do a better job by getting out and talking to patients about their treatment, but you'll also recognize errors sooner.

Know Your Environment

In the health-care field, the better you know the clientele—the patients and their families—the better you can do your job. One of the major complaints about nonmedical personnel in the health-care field is that they don't have a sense of appreciation for the individual patient and focus overly much on the paperwork, forgetting the human element. Let that criticism be a warning of how you might be perceived with a business degree and no health background. You'll need to be concerned about patient welfare and let people know that you are. Take action steps to keep yourself informed of these issues by reading professional journals and newspapers and watching the local news for coverage of health-care issues.

Because health care is undergoing dramatic changes, both in new scientific developments and in its corporate structure, you're going to experience a lot of change in your job. New employees will arrive at your organization to fill new jobs, new forms will appear to meet new needs, and you will encounter new ways of doing things, new products, new techniques, and a constant flow of information. If change is difficult for you on the job, you may find a career in health care a challenge to your peace of mind.

On the other hand, the workday is relatively structured, and most administrative staff have very regular hours. Office spaces are generally attractive. Because you're in health care, where the well-being of the individual is paramount, it's recognized that workplace aesthetics and working conditions make a major contribution to an employee's sense of well-being. Of course, as a salaried worker, you'll probably find there are many times when your day doesn't begin or end with any regularity.

Workplace Risk Issues

There is a myth among the uninitiated that if you work in health care and work in a hospital, you're going to get sick, catch some disease, or generally be more susceptible to infection. Absolutely not! There is no documented evidence that working in a health-care facility in any way increases one's average rate of illness or infection.

Training and Qualifications

As an undergraduate business major, you probably don't have any medical background, other than your own experience as a patient in the medical community (which may be valuable!). You might have had some college or high school courses in physiology or chemistry, but nothing medical or health related. That's OK. Your entry into the world of health care will not depend upon that. You're being hired essentially for your business degree.

Remember what you've read about the volatility of the health-care field. One of the major ingredients in the constant redefinition of health-care delivery is the increasing pressure that exists between the field of medicine and the realm of medical cost containment. Professionals hired on the business side of the equation are well advised to know their stuff! Whether you're looking at sales, finance, systems management, accounting, administration, or facilities management, be prepared to demonstrate, display, and talk about your business education. The prize (a great job) will go to the candidate who knows what he or she's talking about.

Begin a Health-Care Study Program

Your initial attractiveness to the health-care employer will be your potential to cut costs and improve the delivery of patient care. Your competition will be those earning health-care degrees or even those with master's degrees in public health or hospital administration. If you can demonstrate good management skills, a strong goal orientation, and an appreciation of the dynamics of the health-care industry, you'll find the focused generalist (you!) is still a competitive bidder for many entry-level jobs.

While your entry into the field will not depend upon your grasp of the health-care industry, your successful career progress will. Your health-care career will be a sophisticated and complex combination of patient awareness, medical expertise, and economics. You will be learning about each as you progress. More than any other path described in this book, the health-care career path demands that you constantly educate yourself, both on and off the job. On the job, avail yourself of the expertise of those individuals who are more experienced than you are and have them teach you all they can about the profession. Ask for and take advantage of every professional development opportunity your employer makes available to you. Outside of your working hours, keep up with television and press coverage of health-care issues, and read professional journals and magazines to increase your store of information on every aspect of your profession, from disease entities to patient service provisions.

Once you've secured your position and begun your own training program, both formally and informally, your ability to hold your job and to advance in your field will be directly related to your grasp of those larger issues you've been reading about. Eventually in all management jobs, you'll be called upon to concentrate on the more conceptual aspects of your job; e.g., planning and implementing new systems and procedures. This means letting others have responsibility for many of the technical skills and procedures you may have enjoyed and done well. You won't be ready for that change if you haven't taken time to educate yourself along the way in the bigger issues of your industry.

Earnings

You can reasonably expect that in an industry growing as fast as health care the earning power of skilled workers will be correspondingly high and growing. While managerial types in health care (those with business backgrounds) are currently very highly paid, the volatile nature of the industry and the increasing rate of takeovers, mergers, and consolidations of services make earnings very difficult to predict.

While the demographics discussed below would indicate that as the number of people needing health care rises, the value placed on that care and the people who provide it should rise, the correspondingly great pressure from government and private industry to reduce costs may have a dampening effect. There are already situations in state-run health-care facilities where skilled workers are paid less than bus drivers. These discrepancies are being increasingly challenged in the courts under the doctrine of job comparability, which has thus far not received any legal sanction but remains an arguing point in contract negotiations.

Some of the best information about starting salaries in health care is available from the Collegiate Employment Research Institute at Michigan State University. Here are some entry-level salaries for people with undergraduate business degrees pursuing careers in health care that correspond to some of the job postings reviewed earlier in the chapter:

Human resource management	$28,000
Advertising	$34,333
Marketing	$34,000
Financial administration	$42,850

Source: Collegiate Employment Research Institute, Michigan State University.

Career Outlook

Even with the many challenges the industry presents as it seeks to contain costs and provide good care, the career outlook for jobs in the health-care industry is superb. The U.S. Bureau of Labor Statistics predicts that the health services industry will add 2.8 million jobs by 2010—13 percent of total employment growth!

There may only be a small segment of job types among those jobs that you are interested in, but even a small percentage would mean thousands of jobs. Labor Department figures indicate positions for administrators in health care will increase by about 30 percent by the year 2010. Moreover, nine out of twenty of the fastest-growing occupations the Bureau projects are professional and technical health-care jobs. Almost every occupation in health care will have higher-than-average growth through the next decade, including the highly paid managerial positions. Among these occupations, in addition to those that would be attractive to someone with an undergraduate degree in business, there are some that do not require college degrees (home health aides, secretaries, etc.) and some requiring advanced degrees (psychologists, psychometrists, and others).

What has fueled that growth? A number of specific trends, including demographics, technology, changing finances, and home health care.

Changing demographics are a major factor in health-care industry growth. An aging population is aging with better health and more activity than ever before and more income to spend on health maintenance. Those over seventy-five years old, requiring the most medical assistance, will increase by 35 percent over the next two decades. In 1980, the United States achieved the distinction for the first time in history of having slightly more than half its citizenry past the age of thirty. Birth rates and fertility rates remain rather low, but median age continues to climb and remains the single most impactive demographic component of the health-care revolution. A continuously aging society will cause many changes in our future, but the one that concerns us here is the expanded workforce in the health-care field.

The emergence of new technology also affects the health-care industry. Examples of procedures using new technology include reading x-rays long distance, lengthening shortened limbs with external fixation devices, and providing patient-administered analgesics at bedside. As technology proliferates, more services are created and more care opportunities evolve.

Changing finances are another important influence in health care. Talk to people you know who are on a medical coverage plan, and they will tell you they have experienced changes: changes in providers, changes in administration, and especially, changes in cost and who bears that cost. With hospitals forced to deal with cuts in government support, and with the new types of health-care organizations (HMOs and PPOs) growing across the country, management and accounting skills are more highly valued than ever before. We can expect continuing changes in the mix of public and private financing of our health-care system.

Home health care is on the rise, affecting the health-care sector that provides related services. As hospital stays decrease, technology increases, and a patient's confidence in his or her ability to self-manage care continues, the possibilities for what can be done in the patient's home grow.

Strategy for Finding the Jobs

Because your business program has probably not exposed you to the health-care field in any significant way, much of your job search will involve discovering an entire new sector of our economy. If you are like others who have sought employment in the health-care field, you'll find the field very fertile ground for the newly minted business degree student.

I recommend you obtain a good guide to health-care employers, such as *Peterson's Job Opportunities in Health & Science 2000*. This book is readily available to borrow from many college libraries, college career centers, and larger city libraries. It is also available at a modest cost in larger bookstores.

It's a solid resource for two reasons. First, it lists thousands of health-care employers (indexed geographically and alphabetically), and tells you what they do, how many people work for them, and what expertise they may be looking for in new hires. It should expand your horizons about what is possible. For example, perhaps you have some experience in information systems. You probably already realize you can apply at hospitals, larger nursing homes, HMOs, and the traditional sites. Reading through this type of guide, you will begin to recognize other employment opportunities, such as eye-care firms, hospital equipment manufacturers, and pharmaceutical manufacturers.

Expanding your list of possible job sites should be very helpful to you. Each type of employer has its own work environment, its own "climate." Some may suit you more than others. Also, as an entry-level employee with a general business background, you need the flexibility of lots of places to look for entry-level positions in a specialist world such as health care.

You should begin to sort potential employers by hiring needs. Of course, that will help you to locate employers based upon your own talents and career objectives. But it helps in other ways as well. If you are interested in finance, you'll find a long list of employers who generally seek those skills. But, if your job search is localized to a specific geographic area, you can still get some excellent ideas from books like this about the kinds of health-care employers that seek finance skills. Use that information to customize your search to your own geographic area.

Don't overlook state Health and Human Services departments. You might never have thought of those agencies in your own search. While many listings are for federal positions, it's a good bet that your state agency has similar needs. Call the agency and make an appointment to go in and talk to a representative of its human resource department about the agency's expectations for college graduates with interests in finance.

Don't overlook any area of the market:

Assisted living services	Life sciences companies
Biomedical firms	Medical management firms
Dental companies	Medical records management firms
Health maintenance	Medical software firms
organizations	Medical systems
Mental health agencies	Pharmaceutical manufacturers
Hospitals	Physician services
Instrumentation manufacturers	Rehabilitation centers
Insurance companies	Senior citizens' homes
Laboratories	Therapy associates

In examining various sectors of the market, look for job opportunities that fit your expertise. Health care is no different than other areas of employment; it maintains all the essential functions of any business including marketing, sales, administration, finance, accounting, public relations, and all the other traditional business functions.

Because health care is growing so rapidly, you'll encounter many new and smaller firms that are growing rapidly. These firms have leaner staffs and make more use of cross-training. Staff members need to be very flexible and may change jobs frequently as the organization grows. You might want to consider a strategy of affiliating with a smaller, rapidly growing health-care firm. Work hard, learn all you can, and you could find you're riding along with that growth in your own professional advancement.

Here's an eight-step checklist of items to consider in seeking out the best job for you:

1. Check Out Prospective Employers

Everyone in the career field is always suggesting you research the company you are considering. How do you do that? Do you have time to learn to be an employment researcher? Probably not. Start by asking a good reference librarian what you might be able to find out about a company. He or she will suggest everything from stock ratings and Better Business Bureau complaint histories to articles in periodicals. If you can visit the office, park your car outside and observe who comes and goes. What's the building like? Is it attractive and well maintained? How do employees act and dress? Try to arrange an informational interview through the human resources department or the department that is your area of interest. On the day of your appointment, stroll into the lobby (don't worry, nobody will remember you!), look around, ask the receptionist about the firm, and pick up any promotional literature you might find displayed. An on-site visit can be very revealing. If you like what you find, follow up later to track job openings.

2. Display Your Communication Skills

Your résumé, cover letter, thank-you note after an interview, and your manner on the telephone and during an interview are all examples of how you communicate and how you'll do as a communicator for an employer. You'll be judged on that as much as anything. Ensure your written communications are perfect and practice your interviewing skills. Get on the telephone with a friend who will act as the employer in a phone conversation to critique your telemarketing skills. You'll be glad you did.

3. Do You Know a Foreign Language?

It may be too late now to begin a college program, but speaking ability in Spanish would be a real plus in many health-care organizations. Certainly, foreign travel and a sensitivity to other cultures is a valuable experience and one you'll want to talk about, if you can.

4. Prove You Are Results-Oriented

Health care is under the gun and everyone is working hard to produce good results that are economically viable and sensitive to patient and physician needs. In your résumé and during your interview, you want to communicate to the best of your ability that you are a results-oriented person.

5. Add to Your Experience

Going into a field such as health care with a language all its own and a different focus than the kinds of business entities you've studied in college will put some heavy demands on you to grow and add to your experience—quickly. Before that happens, take advantage of your own rich college experience and sample some of the wonderful guest speakers, seminars, and conferences that occur on your campus. Raising your general information level makes you a more valuable employee. You are aware of more issues and can relate more easily to other people through shared ideas and an enhanced appreciation for differing viewpoints. Each learning opportunity of this kind adds to your value to an employer.

6. Network

Chapter 3 of this book described the mechanics of networking. In the health-care field particularly, there are many shared relationships. Professionals in the field share many of the same concerns as health care both grows and changes. You'll meet many fine people during your job search. Regardless of the outcome of those meetings, maintain those relationships and stay interested in those individuals, for they may prove helpful in furthering your job search or in performing your job once you land one.

7. Set Your Job Goals

Health care is a busy field. The business section of a major Boston, Massachusetts, daily recently featured health-care-industry business maneuvers in four of the five front-page stories. With newsworthy changes occurring daily, health care is not an industry where employees will have free time to help you figure out what you want in a job or career. Learn about the industry, learn about the jobs these workers do, and make your own decisions about where you might best fit in. Change your mind as much as you want and as circumstances and information alter your ideas about career paths—but have a plan.

8. Raise Your Level of General Information

Health care is its own field, with its own concerns and issues. You can't change that, but you can change. You can adapt and grow and develop new skills, new talents, and new ways to use your education. By far the best technique to improve your chances of getting hired is to stay abreast of the issues facing health care in this country today. Learning about issues such as length of hospital stay, litigation, medical malpractice and mis-dosing of prescriptions, new advances in radiology, pain, and genetics, and countless other issues will tune you in to the concerns, vocabulary, and players in the health-care game. You'll be guaranteed to draw on this information again and again. Make reading the daily paper a habit!

Common Job Sources

Health care is a big part of our economy, and it is growing faster than other sectors. It should grow by 25 percent through 2010, generating 2.8 million new jobs, according to the U.S. Bureau of Labor Statistics. There are about a quarter of a million health and medical managers who supervise these workers in hospitals, group practice management, long-term care facilities, and doctors' offices. A health-care manager may earn upwards of $60,000, but remember, most top managers have a master's degree. Some smaller facilities hire bachelor's degree holders for managerial positions.

Listed below are just a sampling of the variety of resources available to the health-care job seeker. Begin with these and then move on in your own exploration with the assistance of your career office or reference librarian.

Periodicals with Classifieds
Federal Jobs Digest
Box 594, Department D30
New York, NY 10546
Published biweekly. Up to 30,000 federal job vacancies listed per issue. The federal government employs more than 100,000 health-care workers. Approximately 15,000 health-care job vacancies are projected yearly in the federal government due to retirements. This publication provides comprehensive federal careers articles with each issue.

Hospitals and Health Networks (H&HN)
American Hospital Association
1 N. Franklin
Chicago, IL 60606
Published bimonthly, it has classifieds for a broad spectrum of health-care occupations.

Directories

AHA Guide to the Health Care Field
American Hospital Association with Health Forum Publishing Company
P.O. Box 92683
Chicago, IL 60606
(800) 242-2626
ahaonlinestore.com or healthforum.com
Published annually, this is a comprehensive guide to the health-care field. It
includes information on member hospitals, health-care systems,
organizations, and other valuable information. (Also available on computer
disks.)

American Association of Homes for the Aging
1129 Twentieth St. NW, Suite 400
Washington, DC 20036
aahsa.org
Published annually, this organization's directory lists more than 3,400
member homes and facilities plus 800 suppliers, and individual and
associate members.

*HMO/PPO Directory 2000: U.S. Managed Healthcare Organizations in
Detail Plus Key Decision Makers*, 11th ed. (Montvale, NJ, Medical
Economics, 2000).

Medical and Health Information Directory
Gale Research Company
Book Tower
Detroit, MI 48226
Available at larger libraries, this compendium of resources lists medical
associations, federal government agencies, medical schools, grant-award
sources, health-care delivery agencies, journals, newsletters, and
miscellaneous data.

Possible Job Titles

Account manager	Billing coordinator
Admission marketing director	Billing supervisor

Business manager	Executive director
Collection representative	Home-care contract administrator
Director of services	Manager, media relations
Documentation coordinator	Manager, special events

Note: Allied health-care personnel is a classification of employee you are bound to come across again and again in your job search. Pharmacists, physical therapists, respiratory therapists, x-ray technicians, medical technologists, and occupational therapists are but some examples of the trained, certified, and, in many cases, licensed professions that are included under the rubric *allied health*.

Related Occupations

The issue of related careers is a fascinating subject unto itself. If you've been a surgeon for ten years and decide you no longer want to practice medicine, what can you do? The answer does not lie in the surgical skills, but in the investigative aspect of surgery, in diagnosis and designing solutions to complex problems, and working actively with patients to solve those problems. Counseling, research, and teaching are all skills of the surgeon, but to emphasize those too greatly is to undermine the very dynamic, physical, and realistic part of the surgeon's job that takes place in the operating room.

Leading an outward-bound program or running a halfway house for troubled adolescents would also bring to bear the diagnosis, counseling, and active participation that a surgeon brings to his or her work. In other words, our jobs are often content bound. To do good work, we have to amass information, vocabulary, skills, and facts very specifically related to the content of our jobs. This information very seldom "moves" to other areas of employment, and in the health-care field that may be more true than some other sectors of the economy.

If you look at the health-care industry as a system for providing service to large numbers of people in a sensitive, caring, and highly individualistic way, then you can begin to see the relevance of a career in health care to a career in hotel/restaurant management, which shares many of the same issues. The hospitality industry, in general, hires many individuals who have had careers in health care. The following list of possible employers should be thought of only as a starting point:

Banking/financial services	Mental health services
Community/social work	Museums
Educational institutions	Public relations
Food services	Resorts
Hotel industry	Restaurant management

Professional Associations

One of the preeminent sources of information on careers in health care is the Summit on Manpower, a consortium of eighteen professional health-care groups (including the American Hospital Association).

The Summit on Manpower
1825 K St. NW, Suite 210
Washington, DC 20006

Other helpful associations are listed below, including addresses, any associated training, and publications. Make use of these organizations; their purpose is to foster their professions, and they have a vested interest in raising the quality of employment candidates.

American College of Healthcare Executives
1 N. Franklin, Suite 1700
Chicago, IL 60606-3491
(312) 424-2800
ache.org
Members/Purpose: Works to keep members abreast of current and future trends, issues, and developments and to shape productive and effective organizational strategies and professional performance.
Training: Conducts research programs. Holds educational seminars and training programs on health-care management.
Publications: *Journal of Healthcare Management, Directory, Frontiers of Health Services Management.*

American Medical Association (AMA)
515 N. State St.
Chicago, IL 60610

(312) 464-5000

ama-assn.org

Members/Purpose: County medical societies and physicians. Disseminates scientific information to members and the public. Informs members of significant medical and health legislation at state and national levels and represents the profession before Congress and government agencies. Provides practice counseling for management problems, and keeps membership informed on health and medical legislation.

Publications: *Journal of the American Medical Association (JAMA), American Journal of Diseases of Children, American Medical News, Archives of Dermatology, Archives of General Psychiatry, Archives of Internal Medicine,* and others.

American Public Health Association

800 I St. NW

Washington, DC 20001-3910

(202) 777-2742

apha.org

Members/Purpose: Seeks to protect and promote personal, mental, and environmental health.

Publications: *American Journal of Public Health, The Nation's Health, Salubritas.*

American School Health Association

7263 State Route 43

P.O. Box 708

Kent, OH 44240

(330) 678-1601

Members/Purpose: Promotes comprehensive and constructive school health programs, including the teaching of health, health services, and promotion of a healthful school environment.

Publications: *ASHA Newsletter, Journal of School Health.*

American Society for Health Care Strategy and Market Development

c/o American Hospital Association

One N. Franklin St., 28th Floor

Chicago, IL 60606

(312) 422-3888

Members/Purpose: Persons employed or active in hospitals, hospital councils or associations, hospital-related schools, and health-care organizations responsible for marketing and public relations.

Publications: *Directory of Hospital Marketing, Planning and Public Relations Consultants, Futurescan, Marketing by Numbers, Health Observance Calendar.*

Association of Academic Health Centers
1400 Sixteenth St. NW, Suite 720
Washington, DC 20036
(202) 265-9600
ahcnet.org
Members/Purpose: Chief administrative officers of university-based health centers in the United States. Interdisciplinary in focus, with a primary interest in total health manpower education.
Training: Education programs.
Publications: *Directory*, general meetings.

International Academy of Healthcare Professionals
70 Glen Cove Rd., Suite 209
Roslyn Heights, NY 11577
(516) 621-0620
Members/Purpose: Provides for educational exchange among members. Recognizes outstanding achievement in the health-care field. Offers research and educational materials to third-world health-care institutions.
Training: Provides educational exchange among members.
Publications: Fact sheets and up-to-date news sheets.

**National Association of Health Care
 Career Schools**
750 First St. NE, Suite 940
Washington, DC 20002
nahcs.org
Members/Purpose: Objectives are to promote the interests and general welfare of health career training schools and their students, and to conduct and promote research for the advancement of the educational offerings of such schools.
Publication: *Bulletin.*

National Association for Healthcare Recruitment
P.O. Box 531107
Orlando, FL 32853
(470) 423-4648
nahcr.com
Members/Purpose: Promotes sound principles of professional health-care
recruitment. Provides financial assistance and consultation services.
Training: Conducts regional seminars, symposia, and workshops.
Publications: *Annual Recruitment Survey, Who's Who in Recruitment*
Resources.

National Rural Health Association (NRHA)
1 West Armour Blvd., Suite 203
Kansas City, MO 64111
(816) 756-3140
nrharural.org
Members/Purpose: Purpose is to create a better understanding of health-
care problems unique to rural areas, utilize a collective approach in
finding positive solutions, articulate and represent the health-care needs
of rural America, and supply current information to rural health-care
programs throughout the country.
Training: Offers continuing education credits for medical, dental, nursing,
and management courses.
Publications: *Journal of Rural Health, Rural Health Care.*

9

Path 4: Nonprofits

This chapter advocates a "contrary" strategy in your job search. "Contrarianism" is doing what others are not doing—focusing where the attention isn't. Think of a magician. If you want to figure out what the magician's secret is, don't look to the hand that is drawing your attention. Look at the other hand! While nonprofits may not have been much in evidence during your business education, you may, nevertheless, have heard of the contrarian strategy. Investors use it successfully to find a profitable niche, buying stocks in categories away from where current attention is focused. Focusing on nonprofits in your job search will definitely put you in the minority of job seekers. Let others cling to the older, traditional job search techniques while you explore vast new uncharted opportunities for the business major in a world of enterprise that, at first glance, might seen inimical to your education and outlook.

Who Are the Nonprofits?

Let's begin by defining the nonprofit sector. An easy definition is that it comprises one of the three main sectors of our economy: government, private business, and nonprofits or independents. Here is one of three main sectors of the economy and yet it's seldom addressed in your business education or probably in the advice you've encountered so far in your job search.

What constitutes a nonprofit organization? The obvious first difference is a legal one. Organizations legally termed nonprofit declare that money they receive, or earn, returns to the organization to further its mission and promote its activities and services. It is not returned to investors or owners. Profits, or excess of capital over expenses, may accrue, but they are returned to the activities of the organization.

In legal terms of business incorporation, the nonprofit category (501-c) that designates a nonprofit organization as exempt from taxes by our government covers educational, religious, charitable, scientific, and literary organizations, civic leagues, social welfare organizations, and local employee organizations. If you closely follow the press, you will have noticed a growing number of legal cases challenging the supposed tax-exempt status of many organizations in these areas. This happens as national, state, and local government bodies—increasingly hard-pressed for operating expenses—carefully examine the tax-exempt privileges of those organizations under their purview.

Nonprofits are taking on more and more of the strategies and techniques of the competitive profit sector in order to stay viable. Nonprofits, like any other business enterprise, compete for the public's attention, funds, and goodwill as vigorously as any profit corporation. After all, there's only so much disposable income to go around. If the nonprofits care about what they do, they try as hard as the next organization to grab your attention and your financial support. They use all the same business tools and techniques you have studied in college.

An excellent example of the increasing adoption of strict businesslike management patterns by nonprofits comes from *Mission-Based Management* (2nd ed.; New York: Wiley & Sons, 2000) by Peter C. Brinckerhoff, president of Corporate Alternatives, an Illinois firm specializing in nonprofit organizations. He lists the following attributes of successful nonprofits:

1. A viable mission
2. A businesslike board of directors
3. A strong, well-educated staff
4. Wired and technologically savvy
5. Social entrepreneurs
6. A bias for marketing
7. Financially empowered
8. A vision for where they are going
9. A tight set of controls

This list should sound very familiar to you and should serve as a strong argument for the readiness and willingness of the nonprofit sector to appreciate and value what you have to offer in terms of education and expertise.

Even more important, however, nonprofits offer the kinds of positions, challenges, and projects that a business major would enjoy. There is research and development, marketing, portfolio management, risk analysis, production management, sales, marketing, advertising, training and development—every imaginable facet of the business curriculum has its hands-on application in the world of nonprofit.

Another and far more significant difference in the day-to-day world of work is those underlying principles that animate and motivate the organizations themselves and the people that staff them. Devon Cottrell Smith, in her book *Great Careers: The Fourth of July Guide to Careers, Internships, and Volunteer Opportunities in the Nonprofit Sector* (see Additional Resources section), outlines twelve principles that motivate the creation and continuation of nonprofit organizations:

Vision—inspired action based on a vision of the good.
Harmony—balanced feelings; accord; shared responsibilities; cooperation.
Power—providing resources; the authority to act.
Purification—seeking out hidden problems to effect transformation.
Truth—knowledge of the incontrovertible.
Law—principles on which shared ethics are based.
Love—fidelity to the principle of benevolence.
Foundation—forms that support the function of institutions.
Wisdom—expressing intelligence in life.
Virtue—evolving life through practical adherence to ideas.
Compassion—serving others, providing for basic life needs.
Sustainment—preservation of the social, conceptual, and artistic institutions of society.

Now, take the principles listed above and apply them to some of the pressing issues of today, such as:

- AIDS research
- African drought patterns
- Preserving natural resources
- Containing pollution
- Fostering the arts
- Organizing people for group strength
- Harmonizing extremes of wealth and poverty
- Attending to homelessness and hunger
- Encouraging diversity and tolerance

You can begin to see very clearly why organizations with these principles and these missions need the finest in business management techniques. Sadly, the concerns of many nonprofits are not uppermost in the minds of people. Some of that indifference accounts for the little time spent on nonprofit organizations in business schools. The goals of nonprofits are critical to our viability as a planet, however. To stay competitive, many of these organizations have realized that concepts such as total quality management (TQM), strategic planning, work flow management, business communications, database information systems, and so on are critical. Business majors interested in the goals of the nonprofits provide the essential cutting-edge skills these organizations need to survive.

A third big difference is organizational culture. Most nonprofits do their work in a "life-friendly" work culture. Some of this rejection of workaholism has to do with not being profit-focused and some with the caring, nurturing focus of many of the organizational missions themselves. Some evidence of this is in the heavy emphasis on professional training and development, allowing time off for college courses, workshops, community volunteering, and sabbaticals. Nonprofits recognize the value of workers recharging, meeting new people, and acquiring new skills.

Definition of the Career Path

There are many wonderful opportunities for the business major in the nonprofit sector. There are so many career pathways, in fact, that starting down one is apt to open up vistas of ever-widening opportunity. Nonprofits will surprise and delight the business major with the variety and number of job opportunities available.

Most nonprofit organizations share certain common departments, however. The following descriptions will give you an idea of the duties and responsibilities of those departments and positions and the qualifications needed for them. Within each department there are numerous career paths possible as you grow in experience and training. Each of these areas has been illustrated with excerpts from a recent advertisement for that job, so you can see and read for yourself how employers express their needs in these areas.

Executive Director

Duties. This position is called many things: dean, managing director, hospital administrator, chief executive officer, and so on. Responsibilities include directing the overall program and administrative activities of the organization and the effective use of financial and human resources. In smaller nonprofits, the executive director and a small support staff may be the only full-time employees. In larger organizations, the executive director's office is comprised of an extensive staff, all with different responsibilities.

Qualifications. Executive directors today often have an M.B.A. or M.P.A. (master's in public administration). However, there are still people rising to executive director positions who have come up "through the ranks" with an undergraduate business degree and the winning combination of drive, enthusiasm, and dedication.

Development Officer
Duties. This is the department that raises money to support the organization's day-to-day as well as long-term needs for paying staff salaries and financing new initiatives, programs, or even facilities. The shrinking tradition of philanthropy in this country, the slow erosion of government support, and the increasing contention for what is left of our discretionary income make the role of this department both a central and a challenging one. The more successful this department is, the more growth the organization can accomplish.

Qualifications. A business major will find much of the activity of this office familiar. There is a strong sales orientation, and much time and effort is spent on marketing the organization to potential supporters. Direct mail campaigns and database technology are valuable tools, as is creativity in developing marketing concepts, promotions, and premiums (gifts). Most of this job is learned as you go, but basic requirements include organizational ability, concern for the world and people, and the willingness to make a commitment. Skills in writing and research are often useful, and the personal qualities of confidence, articulateness, initiative, and curiosity are helpful.

Working Conditions

How will working in a nonprofit differ from working somewhere else? You'll sense a different atmosphere because the operative motivation is different. In business, the goal is "gain," i.e., money. There's certainly nothing wrong with that, and if the business or service is supplying people with something they want or need, financial profit is the direct and expected result of a well-managed enterprise. Without that profit, the commercial firm cannot continue to provide what the public wants. If you had a favorite restaurant, think how disappointed you'd be to hear it had closed because it hadn't charged diners enough to sustain its continued existence.

In nonprofits, the emphasis is on the cause, not the reward mechanism. People in nonprofits tend to have bigger, more idealistic goals and see the work they do as part of a larger movement of good for society and the world as a whole.

The implications of this difference in focus are far ranging. There's less "What's in it for me" in workers' attitudes, less competitiveness in the office, and more emphasis on the big picture, not the bottom line. Some generalizations about staff extending themselves, being kinder to each other, and being more aware of the global implications of political, economic, and governmental machinery would probably not be very far off the mark.

There is an ample body of literature, films, and television dramas about workers and executives getting fed up with jobs that revolve around producing, selling, or convincing people to buy a never-ending stream of products. While nonprofits have their own share of frustrations, the goals and missions seldom are the cause of boredom or tedium on the part of workers.

This is important work, done in a spirit of cooperation, even fun. There is generally a lower stress level, because many of the superficial aspects of for-profit firms are missing—fancy clothes, expensive cars, and all the other accoutrements of a profit-based workplace. Nonprofits do sometimes complain about the quality and condition of their workplaces and technology, but they are also resourceful and enterprising in accomplishing their goals. Many people in nonprofits speak of a more relaxed pace and less pressure. They feel more flexibility to do many more jobs and hold greater amounts of responsibility than they might in a larger, more structured corporate world.

Training and Qualifications

Your college education is important to nonprofits, but even more important may be your interest in some particular segment of the nonprofit sector and any past experience in that area. This kind of experience substantiates your stated goals and ensures those hiring you that you understand and have a realistic picture of the work you're getting into. If you haven't yet graduated, consider spending a summer in an internship or devoting extra hours during the school year to volunteer work. This may even be worth your while after graduation if you can manage it.

For example, community service jobs are highly diverse, from medical services and social work to the organization of neighborhood efforts to defeat crime or drug traffic. Large housing services in cities have staffs that do nothing but manage property and lend money for construction. Your college degree may get you in the door, but to leave the interview with people still interested in you, you'll need to educate yourself to understand what they do and be able to express a well-reasoned explanation for not only why you want to join them but where you see yourself fitting in.

The arts are one of the major subgroups of nonprofit employers. Here you'll find you're up against the infamous "You need experience, but I can't give it to you" catch-22. Entry-level jobs in arts organizations are tough to get and there is great competition. You may have to begin in a lower-level job to gain entry and work your way up in the organization through internal promotions. Or, you might approach the arts organization with a résumé that relates your experience in another area to your interest in the arts. For example, if you've done fund-raising or special event planning, you might begin by knocking on the doors of the development offices of nonprofit theatres, symphony orchestras, or art galleries.

The environmental subgroup is so popular that hiring demands there are very competitive, requiring not only technical expertise but an understanding of specific environmental issues at a sophisticated level and the ability to advocate for change. If you are interested in the environment and lack a specialty degree, start locally as an intern or volunteer while in school and then begin your job search with state or regional groups. Some business-related jobs are listed at the websites sustainablebusiness.com and eco.org.

Museums and other preservationist organizations look for a college education, some practical experience, and an understanding on the part of the applicant that these organizations have all kinds of work: membership services, security, curatorship, display and mounting, preservation and curating, marketing, sales, and public relations. Many of those are appropriate for a business major, and if you have a background in art, there are more possibilities.

Earnings

Approximately half of current operating expenditures in nonprofit organizations are spent on employee compensation. Most historic data indicate that wages and salaries in the sector were 74 percent of average wages and salaries in all other sectors of the economy in 1990, an increase from 73 percent in

1989. In 2002, average nonprofit sector CEOs made $73,000, much less than their for-profit sector counterparts, according to Abbot, Langer and Associates. Some made much more than this average, of course.

There's a curious dichotomy about salaries in the nonprofit sector that you should be aware of. On the one hand, nonprofits realize that to be successful and to attract the talent they need (that includes you!), they have to offer competitive salaries and benefits. On the other hand, many staff members are attracted to the organization largely because of its goals and orientation and derive some "psychic" income in that way. For some employers, this is rationalization enough to set salary levels somewhat lower than is competitive. Both situations occur with mind-boggling regularity in the nonprofit sector. It varies from one organization to the next. Let's compare two similar position descriptions for similar organizations in our nation's capital, taken from *Community Jobs*, that illustrate the Jekyll and Hyde situation of compensation. Both of these jobs in organizations of similar size and funding are for program coordinators, a common nonprofit job title that refers to individuals who develop and coordinate education, advocacy, and organization plans for an organization. They attend meetings, publish newsletters, and attempt to build an activist base of volunteers to accomplish goals. It's an important job but can come with very different levels of rewards:

JOB A

Program Coordinator: Proven organizing skills with national organization, excellent writing and editing ability. Team builder. $29,000 salary.

JOB B

Program Coordinator: Proven leadership ability and supervisory skills, and the ability to motivate others and achieve goals. Mid- to upper 30s.

The full descriptions show these two positions are very similar in scope and demands and yet the possibility of a $10,000 difference in salary, in the same city, exists. This is a frequent situation in nonprofits and something you need to stay aware of.

While high earnings may not be what working for a not-for-profit organization is about, on the other hand, you need to be realistic about your financial needs—now, and into the future. Salaries are an important and frequently discussed issue for all who choose to work in nonprofits.

Relationship to Budget

At the end of this section I have listed some general reference works on salary data in the nonprofit sector. Because information may be hard to find, one of the ways I have become proficient at estimating salary levels is by regularly and closely reading job ads for nonprofit sector employment. It remains my most valuable primary source of compensation information.

However, another very logical way to come to an understanding of possible salary levels is to work down from the chief executive salary to your level of management. A 2002 survey by *Board and Administrator* (Frederick, MD: Aspen Publishers) provided the information in Table 9.1 on average executive director salaries compared to budget size. But individual chief executive salaries vary dramatically, depending upon the experiential history of the incumbent. In past surveys, *Board and Administrator* cited a $20,000 difference between an incumbent with more than fifteen years of nonprofit employment history at a senior level and one with less than five years' experience. Obviously, one would expect these differentials for experience would translate to lower levels, as well (see Table 9.2).

TABLE 9.1: 2002 NONPROFIT EXECUTIVE COMPENSATION

Organizational Budget	Average Salary of Chief Exceecutive
$0–250,000	$40,098
$250,001–500,000	$45,345
$500,001–1 million	$56,682
$1 million–1.5 million	$64,265
$1.5 million–2 million	$63,006
$2 million–2.5 million	$72,664
$2.5 million–3 million	$76,011
$3 million–4 million	$77,500
$4 million–5 million	$77,086
$5 million–6 million	$79,252
$6 million–10 million	$91,645
More than $10 million	$108,215

Source: 2002 Aspen Publishers, Inc.

TABLE 9.2: NOT-FOR-PROFIT COMPENSATION AND BENEFITS: 2002 AVERAGE SALARY

Position	<$5m	$5–$9.9m	$10–$19.9m	$20–$49.9m	$50–$99.9m	>$100m
			Operating Budget Size			
Chief Executive Officer	$102,227	$165,337	$196,637	$219,992	$241,744	$370,602
Chief Operating Officer	$74,826	$96,371	$146,079	$141,547	$170,317	$246,670
Top Financial	$62,655	$87,989	$104,076	$109,120	$126,685	$185,778
Controller	$47,114	$62,042	$65,929	$72,467	$88,249	$120,577
Top Marketing	$60,567	$82,872	$99,090	$96,174	$116,114	$156,505
Top Information Systems	$40,386	$81,975	$86,042	$106,464	$108,757	$165,814
Top Public Relations	—	$51,687	$82,015	$78,505	$101,910	$120,502
Top Administration	—	$73,873	—	$111,641	$140,911	$154,502
Top Membership	—	$47,260	—	$67,481	$84,487	$114,061
Top Publications	—	—	$88,657	$89,263	$89,508	$110,482
Top Grant Administration	—	—	$62,020	—	$66,509	$77,769
Top Development	$60,376	$100,319	$103,423	$100,962	$114,145	$161,065

Note: dash (—) indicates insufficient data
Source: Buck Consultants/Mellon Financial. Not-for-Profit Compensation and Benefits 2002 survey.

Other Forms of Compensation

Benefits are one way to add to an employee's package of compensation without as direct an outlay of funds as simple salary. Nonprofits are competitive in regard to benefits with their private sector counterparts, as reported in *Board and Administrator*'s survey that divides nonprofits into small budgets (less than $500,000) and large budgets ($6 million and more). Note: these benefits are as reported for executive directors.

PERCENTAGE OF NONPROFITS OFFERING SELECTED BENEFITS

	Small Budget	Large Budget
Health insurance	74%	96%
Life insurance	49%	87%
Retirement	42%	90%
Dental	33%	63%
Disability insurance	32%	60%
Education assistance	21%	43%

Resources on Nonprofit Compensation

Association Staff Compensation and Benefits Study
   (national summary)
American Society of Association Executives
1575 I St. NW
Washington, DC 20005-1168

Board and Administrator: 2002 Report on Nonprofit
   Executive Director Compensation
Aspen Publishers, Inc.
7201 McKinney Cir.
Frederick, MD 21704
(800) 234-1660

Compensation in Nonprofit Organizations (14th ed.)
Abbott, Langer and Associates
548 First St.
Crete, IL 60417
(708) 672-4200

Compensation in Not-for-Profit Organizations
Coopers & Lybrand/Survey Research Unit
1301 Avenue of the Americas
New York, NY 10019-6013
(212) 259-2447

1994 Wage and Benefit Survey of Northern California
Nonprofit Organizations
The Management Center
870 Market St., Suite 800
San Francisco, CA 94102-2903

Not-for-Profit Employment from the 1990 Census of Population and
Housing (Preliminary Findings)
Independent Sector
1828 L St. NW
Washington, DC 20036
(202) 223-8100

Career Outlook

We are all worried about our working future, and this chapter opened with some troublesome examples of the changing face of employment opportunities in this country. As the global economy moves into the information age, there seem to be fewer traditionally "prime" jobs and more jobs in the low-paying sectors, many of them only "temp" or part-time positions. Those who have tried to comfort us claim the desirability of a greatly reduced work-week that will allow people to pursue private pleasures or socially useful projects. Before this comes about, however, we will as a nation have to come to terms with a future in which the traditional place of private sector jobs no longer holds center stage in our economic and social life.

If you are considering the nonprofit arena as a good place to make a career and find value for your business degree, you may also find you have chosen the one sector of the economy where the opportunities won't diminish over time. In his 1995 book *The End of Work: The Decline of the Global Labor Force and the Dawn of the Post-Market Era* (New York: G.P Putnam's Sons), author and activist Jeremy Rifkin says that whether the issue is health care for an aging population, preservation of our nation's treasures, developing community projects, or fostering the arts, it is these person-to-person, nurturing skills that will be least vulnerable to replacement by computers, robots, bar scanners, and telecommunications technology. Scan the job-listing pages of a publication such as *Community Jobs* and try to reduce the job announcements listed there to digitalization or computerization. You cannot! These jobs are too complex, too difficult, requiring intimate contact between people. Though your role in these organizations may not be on the front lines of client/customer contact, it is the nonprofit organizations and their missions that will be among the elite, status-invested jobs of the future.

Already, we see the beginnings of a society with more of an emphasis on helping others. Your own college probably had an office of volunteer services that placed college students in community service sites such as senior centers, animal shelters, halfway houses, environmental clean-up projects, and other similar endeavors. Your high school or even grade school may have encouraged similar events and outreach for students. This trend is occurring as we as a nation learn of our citizenship with all peoples and our connection to the entire ecosystem of our planet.

An encouraging trend for nonprofits has been the growing number of for-profit firms that are "adopting" and sponsoring the efforts of nonprofits. Several things are indicated by this corporate interest. First, the valuable work of nonprofits is increasingly recognized and supported by the establishment. This corporate funding allows them to continue their work. Second, the corporations themselves become vested with some of the "halo" of good works that cloaks the nonprofits they sponsor, and that is, of course, good for business. Third, and most important, through the publicity of the corporation the nonprofit gains a far wider and more appreciative audience than it could on its own efforts.

Strategy for Finding the Jobs

Let's outline a smart three-step strategy to determine the best possible use of your skills in the nonprofit sector. As you work your way through these steps, you'll need to devote ample time to the completion of these activities. You'll need to think about your choices and to meet and talk with people regarding the various possibilities. Essentially, the strategy involves three steps: making some important decisions, talking to people, and focusing your efforts. Let's take each step by itself

Step I Make Three Decisions
First of all, realize your job search in the nonprofit sector is not very different from any other job search. You'll need to begin by focusing your energy and your efforts so you aren't overwhelmed by information and options. The

areas you can begin to make some decisions include identifying what kinds of nonprofits you want to seek out, where you want to work, and how you will be positioning yourself as a candidate, based on your education and skills.

Let's consider the factors involved in these decisions:

1. **Be certain you believe in the mission.** Nonprofits revolve around a mission more intensely than do many profit organizations. Whether the mission is aid to refugees, irrigation education, protection of abused children, equal justice, fair employment, or any of the thousands of other objectives, it should be something you are interested in and can remain interested in during your career. When it comes to hiring, nonprofits seek to establish the level of your commitment and the rationale for it. Understand their issues and decide which issues you most believe in and which might best sustain your enthusiasm, interest, and passion.

2. **Determine where you want to work.** This chapter has demonstrated an enormous variety of nonprofit jobs and a corresponding variety of work sites, from China to the inner city. What appeals to you? Are your concerns localized to your own town or city or your own state or region of the country? Are your concerns localized to a particular region of the United States, such as the Great Plains or the timberlands of the Northwest? Are you interested in South America, Asia, or Africa? Or do you want to be involved in a global issue involving the whole of the planet and our impact upon it? Answers to these questions will have much to do with not only the kind of organization you affiliate with, but also where that organization is located and where its operations are focused.

3. **Position yourself to fit into the organization.** Even within a particular niche of the nonprofits, there can be major differences in how people go about their work. Say, for example, you have selected the arts as an area you feel will sustain your career interests. Within the arts there are arts advocates, lobbyists, policy makers, educators, and a host of other positions, all requiring very different skills and using different ways of communicating and working together.

It's not a potential employer's job to figure out how you'll fit in the operation. You need to understand what that organization does and how you might best make a contribution to its mission. To make a winning presentation, use Chapter 1, "The Self-Assessment," to analyze your skills and attributes, to reflect on your personality and work style, and to understand your communication preferences. Prepare yourself to present pertinent information about yourself to interviewers in a way they can appreciate. For example, if you are seeking a position with the Public Broadcasting Service (PBS), you should be aware that its activities include program acquisition and scheduling, educational services, advertising and promotion, audience research, broadcast and technical operations, development (fund-raising), and engineering. If your strong skills are marketing/advertising and you have some good computer skills, you could look at opportunities in audience research and consumer behavior, or advertising and promotion, or special events and fund-raising and promotion activities.

Step 2 Get Out and Meet People in Nonprofits

Start by meeting people who are working in your preferred nonprofit field in your own community area and then network out in increasingly wide circles to develop relationships with other professionals in this field. For example, perhaps your interest is in the environment, or more specifically, preserving natural wetlands and forest from development. Begin with your town administrators or planning board. Perhaps they belong to a national program that fosters the planting and replacement of lost trees in a community and provides grants for that purpose. Contacting national organizations can often lead you to more statewide contacts in the specific areas of your interest.

The Great Jobs series repeatedly stresses the advantages of using your school's alumni network to meet people in your field. Some students prefer to contact alumni because they already share the same college experience and because alumni often have more commitment to helping students from their own schools than do other people you may encounter. Certainly, my clients return again and again with stories of making instant friends with alumni in our network. They remark on the candor of our alumni contacts and the detailed information they are willing to provide. This process will help you find more contacts, more employment sites, and will also refine your interview content because as you search out your network, you learn more and more about the job, yourself, and how you can make the best fit between the two.

Review the chapter on networking (Chapter 3) to ensure you make the most out of every meeting. It will tell you how to prepare for each meeting and how to conduct interviews. It provides you with a variety of sample questions and explains how to follow up in order to keep your various contacts alive and fresh.

Step 3 Focus Your Search

Since you are spending significant time and money in a job search, you should narrow down your search and be more targeted. To accomplish that, you should do the following:

- Determine the type of mission(s) you are most interested in.
- Decide on the geographic area of your search.
- Determine one or two positions to seek in these organizations.
- Set thresholds for entry-level income.

In all likelihood, your final focus will be some blend of these four factors. Even with this starting focus, each informational interview will increase your knowledge in several ways. You'll learn the special vocabulary of the field, the unique challenges of the geographic location you've chosen, and you'll increasingly grasp the nature of the job you've targeted so that you become a sharper, more defined candidate.

Possible Employers

A taxonomy developed by Dr. Michael O'Neill divides the nonprofits into eleven categories:

1. Human and social service organizations
2. Mutual benefit organizations
3. Business, professional, farming, and labor organizations
4. Religious organizations
5. Scientific research organizations
6. Legislative, legal, political, and advocacy organizations
7. Health service organizations
8. Arts, cultural, historical, and community-educational organizations
9. Community development organizations
10. Private nonprofit educational organizations
11. Grant-making organizations

You will find an abundance of material that you can use to locate possible employers in the nonprofit sector. Let's examine these resources in order, from the most general to the most specific.

General Descriptive Sources
The reference works listed below are a good beginning because they give you a broad overview of the narrow areas of the nonprofit sector, how these organizations are structured, and what kind of employees populate them. Many of these resources will identify specific job titles and the duties and responsibilities associated with those positions, as well as the personal characteristics of the people chosen to fill them.

America's Top Internet Job Sites: Finding a Job Online, by Ron and Caryl Krannich (Manassas Park, VA: Impact Publications, 2001).

Doing Well by Doing Good: The Complete Guide to Careers in the Non Profit Sector, by Terry W. McAdam (New York: Doubleday, 1988). (Now out of print, though still available in libraries and worth the search.)

Finding a Job in the Nonprofit Sector (Farmington Hills: The Taft Group, 1991).

From Making a Profit to Making a Difference, by Richard King (River Forest, IL: Planning/Communications, 2000).

Harvard Business School Guide to the Nonprofit Sector, by Stephanie Lowell (Boston: Harvard Business School Press, 2000).

Nonprofits' Job Finder, by Daniel Lauber (River Forest, IL: Planning Communications, new edition forthcoming 2003).

100 Best Nonprofits to Work For, 2nd ed., by Leslie Hamilton and Robert Tragert (Lawrenceville, NJ: Thomson Learning, 2000).

100 Jobs in the Environment, by Debra Quintana (New York: Macmillan, 1996).

Directories

These excellent reference works are widely available and list organizations by type, by job category, and by geographic location. Many also contain bibliographies and resource lists that will offer additional, more specific information.

Alternatives to the Peace Corps: Gaining Third World Experience, by Becky Buell and Kam Harnerschiag (Oakland, Institute for Food & Development Policy, 1994).

Directory of Internships in Youth Development (1993)
The National Collaboration for Youth
1319 F St. NW, Suite 601S
Washington, DC 20004

Food First Books
Institute for Food and Development Policy
398 60th St.
Oakland, CA 94618-1212

The Foundation Directory, 24th ed. (New York: Foundation Center, 2002).

Good Works: A Guide to Careers in Social Change, ed. by Jessica Cowan (New York: Barricade Books, 1991).

Great Careers: The Fourth of July Guide to Careers, Internships, and Volunteer Opportunities in the Non-Profit Sector, ed. by Devon Cottrell Smith (Garrett Park, MD: Garrett Park Press, 1990).

National Directory of Nonprofit Organizations (Detroit: The Taft Group, 1997).

The Peace Corps and More: 114 Ways to Work, Study, and Travel in the 3rd World, by Medea Benjamin (San Francisco: Global Exchange, 1991).

Job Listings

For a career counselor like me, the list below is as familiar and important as a group of good friends. We use these resources in the office daily as they are excellent sources of information on potential career opportunities for college graduates seeking to enter the nonprofit sector. Check them out. If your career center doesn't subscribe to them, check your college or university library or a major city library nearby. Your own college career center may be able to arrange for you to use the services of another college that does subscribe through professional reciprocity. The hunt will be worth it.

Once you locate these job listings, use them to their best advantage. Any issue tells you far more than simply what jobs are currently available. There is editorial content that will inform you about current issues in the field, legislative initiatives, ethical challenges, and interesting profiles of nonprofit professionals. Read the back issues, too, and you'll expand your awareness of job titles, job sites, and even possible salary figures. These job postings lists can teach you about job sites you might not have considered, and even though a job listing may be very old, if the job looks attractive to you, explore similar nonprofits to ascertain their needs for that kind of employee.

American Association of Museums
1575 Eye St. NW, Suite 400
Washington, DC 20005
(202) 289-1818
Fax: (202) 289-6578
aam-us.org

Art Search: The National Employment Service Bulletin for the Performing Arts
Theater Communications Group
355 Lexington Ave.
New York, NY 10017
tcg.org

Arts Opportunities
The Career Planning and Placement Office
The Maryland Institute College of Art
1300 W. Mount Royal Ave.
Baltimore, MD 21217
mica.edu/careernews

**Association for
   Experiential Education**
2885 Aurora, #28
Boulder, CO 80303-2252
aee.org

The Chronicle of Philanthropy
P.O. Box 1989
Marion, OH 43305
philanthropy.com

Environmental Careers Organization
179 South St.
Boston, MA 02111
(617) 426-4375
eco.org

Environmental Opportunities
P.O. Box 670
Walpole, NH 03608

HandsNet
20195 Stevens Creek Blvd., Suite 120
Cupertino, CA 95104
(408) 257-4500
handsnet.org
HandsNet is a national network of resources for social and economic
change. Network tools include *Federal Register* abstracts covering education;
the OnLine News Clipping Service, which provides daily news briefs
covering human services and justice topics; and fax capability. HandsNet's
public forums on key human service issues are open to all members.
Organizations with regional or national memberships can develop private
forums to facilitate group work.

Idealist.org
A nonprofit career center is one of the services of this site, a project of the group Action Without Borders. The site has an international focus on nonprofit organizations.

Independentsector.org
This site has information on many organizations in the nonprofit or independent sector. A job link is maintained by this group, whose purpose is to promote and foster nonprofit service organizations and philanthropic activity.

Institute for
  Global Communications (IGC)
18 DeBoom
San Francisco, CA 94107
(415) 442-0220
igc.org
The Institute for Global Communications (IGC) offers four computer networks: ConflictNet, EcoNet, LaborNet, and PeaceNet. ConflictNet provides telecommunications services to professionals and volunteers who work with organizations that promote peaceful resolution of disputes. EcoNet links people and organizations that work for environmental causes. LaborNet is the newest IGC network and provides information to labor representatives. PeaceNet connects activists and organizations involved in working for peace and human rights issues.

The Job Seeker
  (environmental jobs)
Route 2, Box 16
Warrens, WI 54666

National Organization
  for Women
733 Fifteenth St. NW, Suite 240
Washington, DC 20005
(202) 628-8669 ext. 145
Local chapters have career information and links. National organization focuses on issues of interest to women, including career advancement and equal pay.

**New York Foundation
for the Arts**
155 Avenue of the Americas,
14th Floor
New York, NY 10013-1507
(212) 366-6900
Fax: (212) 366-1778
nyfaweb@nyfa.org

The Nonprofit Times
Executive Offices
120 Littleton Rd., Suite 120
Parsippany, NJ 07054-1803
(973) 394-1800
Fax: (973) 394-2888
nptimes.com

Nonprofits.gov
Government website gathers together information about federal government
resources for use by nonprofit organizations doing research and fund-
raising. Management resources, research and policy resources are
highlighted with links to many government sites.

Nonprofits.org
This website contains general information about the nonprofit sector and
resources for further research. Run by the Internet Nonprofit Center and
the Evergreen State Society.
INC
c/o P.O. Box 20682
Seattle, WA 98102-0682
nonprofits.org

*Opportunities in
Public Affairs*
Brubach Enterprises
P.O. 34349
Bethesda, MD 20827
(301) 571-0102
opajobs.com

PNNOnline
3313 West Cary St.
Richmond, VA 23221
(804) 342-7665
Fax: (804) 342-8015
pnnonline.org
Philanthropy News Network (PNN) follows events in the charitable giving sector. Also maintains a career center online with job listings. Publishes twice-weekly E-mail news alert.

The WELL (Whole Earth 'Lectronic Link)
27 Gate Five Rd.
Sausalito, CA 94965
(415) 332-6106

Whole Earth **Magazine**
1408 Mission Ave.
San Rafael, CA 94901
(415) 256-2800
info@wholeearthmag.com
wholeearth.org

Possible Job Titles

Many job titles in the nonprofit sector are indistinguishable from the world of commercial, for-profit jobs. There are chief executive officers, marketing directors, nurses, doctors, lawyers, and more. We examined some positions earlier in this chapter that held job titles a business major could easily identify and appreciate. But there are some job titles unique to the world of nonprofits. Many are listed below. In every case these are positions that are appropriate for people with business degrees.

Canvass director	Fund-raiser
Case manager	Major donor field representative
Communications assistant	Outreach worker
Community organizer	Political activist
Energy advocate	Research assistant
Farm apprentice	Tenant organizer
Field assistant	Union organizer

Related Occupations

By now, the direct correlations between nonprofit and for-profit organizations have been made clear more than once. The reader of this chapter should understand that not only are many jobs the same, many nonprofits have looked to the profit sector for management guidance and strategic initiatives. Goals of profit may be vastly different, but both profit and nonprofit organizations realize that only well-managed organizations survive.

We have also seen that many nonprofits have created for-profit subsidiaries to generate income for their nonprofit initiatives. Many nonprofit museums, for example, have found a ready market and significant revenues through selling fine art and reproductions of museum pieces in museum stores, incorporated as for-profit subsidiaries and often administered by outside vendors. Profits are returned to the museum as income to support new museum ventures. This lessens some of the risks inherent in depending upon money from grants or the support of the public for all of a museum's funding.

A Sample of Some Larger Nonprofit Organizations

This is a selected list, taken from the *National Directory of Nonprofit Organizations*, 15th ed. (Rockville, MD: The Taft Group, 2002).

American Ballet (New York City)
American Council for Nationalities Service (New York City)
American Enterprise Institute for Public Policy Program (D.C.)
American Film Institute (D.C.)
American Indian Heritage Foundation (Falls Church, Virginia)
American Philosophical Society (Philadelphia, Pennsylvania)
American Printing House for the Blind (Louisville, Kentucky)
American Society for the Prevention of Cruelty to Animals (New York City)
Amnesty International of the USA (New York City)
Association for Women in Science (D.C.)
Campaign for Human Development (D.C.)
Cancer Care (New York City)
Carnegie Council on Ethics and International Affairs (New York City)
Chicago Historical Society (Chicago, Illinois)
Children's Hospital (Columbus, Ohio)
Children's Television Workshop (New York City)
Common Cause (D.C.)
Cooperative for American Relief Everywhere International (CARE) (New York City)

Courage Center (Golden Valley, Minnesota)

Cousteau Society (Norfolk, Virginia)

Environmental Defense Fund (New York City)

Ethics and Public Policy Center (D.C.)

Food for the Hungry (D.C.)

Friends of the Earth (D.C.)

Gray Panthers (D.C.)

International Prison Ministry (Dallas, Texas)

Lawyers Committee for Civil Rights Under Law (D.C.)

Literacy Volunteers of America (Syracuse, New York)

Metropolitan Opera Guild (New York City)

Mothers Against Drunk Driving (MADD) (Hurst, Texas)

National Committee for the Prevention of Child Abuse
    (Chicago, Illinois)

Nature Conservancy (Arlington, Virginia)

Outward Bound USA (Greenwich,
    Connecticut)

Partners for Livable Places (D.C.)

Pro Football Hall of Fame (Canton, Ohio)

Resources for the Future (D.C.)

Save the Children (Westport, Connecticut)

Sierra Club (San Francisco, California)

UNICEF (New York City)

Union of Concerned Scientists (Cambridge,
    Massachusetts)

United Negro College Fund (New York City)

United Way of America (Alexandria, Virginia)

Volunteers of America (Metairie, Louisiana)

Wilderness Society (D.C.)

YMCA, YWCA (New York City)

Professional Associations

Professional associations remain a seldom-used but immensely valuable tool for job seekers. The organizations listed below have a vested interest in raising your level of general information about the career fields they represent. Most are very generous with their publications and providing answers to questions. Give them a try.

Alliance for Nonprofit Management
1899 L St. NW, 6th Floor
Washington, DC 20036
(202) 955-8406
Members/Purpose: Seeks to further education and leadership capabilities in order to enhance both individuals and the management of the nonprofit organization.
Training: Provides opportunity to further education through information sharing and networking among members.

Association for Research on Nonprofit Organizations and Voluntary Actions
550 W. North St.
Indianapolis, IN 46202-3162
(317) 684-2120
arnova.org
Members/Purpose: Stimulates, coordinates, and aids the efforts of those engaged in voluntary action research, scholarship, and professional activity.
Training: Sponsors collaborative research proposals and projects on voluntary action topics.
Publication: *ARNOVA Newsletter.*

BoardSource
1828 L Street NW, Suite 900
Washington, DC 20036-5114
Members/Purpose: Building effective nonprofit boards. Seeks to improve the effectiveness of nonprofit organizations in fields such as arts and culture, conservation, religion, youth development, public policy, health and medicine, and social welfare by strengthening their governing boards.
Training: Offers assistance in organizing training programs, workshops, and seminars for nonprofit organizations.
Publications: Books and booklets, makes available audiotapes.

Society for Nonprofit Organizations
6314 Odana Rd., Suite 1
Madison, WI 53719
(608) 274-9777

Members/Purpose: Provides a forum for the exchange of information, knowledge, and ideas on strengthening and increasing productivity within nonprofit organizations and among their leaders.

Training: Sponsors seminars and workshops on nonprofit management and leadership.

Publications: *National Directory of Service and Product Providers, Nonprofit World: The National Nonprofit Leadership and Management Journal, Society for Nonprofit Organizations—Resource Center Catalog.*

Volunteer Trustees of Not-for-Profit Hospitals
818 Eighteenth St. NW, Suite 900
Washington, DC 20006

Members/Purpose: Objectives are to provide a trustee voice in policy making and legislative activities, and develop a communication network among trustees in order to provide the highest quality medical care at the lowest possible price.

Path 5: Research Associate

A Strategic Approach to the M.B.A.

While you're in college majoring in business, you are going to hear the M.B.A. (master of business administration) degree mentioned frequently. Many of your professors will have received this degree on the way to their doctoral work in business. It has probably been frequently mentioned in your business textbooks, case studies, and profiles of successful businesswomen and men.

Not all M.B.A. degrees are created equal, however, and M.B.A. programs, curricula, and faculty can vary dramatically from school to school. The M.B.A. degree has come under considerable scrutiny in the past ten years, and there have been many news stories and journal articles discussing the increasing proliferation of M.B.A. programs and the lack of quality in some of their program offerings, especially those from smaller schools. M.B.A. programs are frequently evaluated and rated in the business press, and it is understood there is no comparison between the M.B.A. degree offered by one of the larger, top ten programs in the country, with a dedicated graduate faculty, and the offerings of a small, private, or state-supported college whose undergraduate faculty may be doing double duty in both the M.B.A. program and undergraduate classes.

Nevertheless, the M.B.A. degree has much to offer the qualified business major and, in most instances, the degree can enhance your career. M.B.A. programs place a high value on prior work experience when it comes to assessing the admission applications of a new class. Those employers that hire the graduates of M.B.A. programs put an equally high premium on work experience. Some of that high salary the M.B.A. earns in many cases is a reward for that expected experience. Would you want to be treated by a physician who had read all the right books but never had any patient contact before meeting you? Of course not! The M.B.A. is no different than any other professional degree. There is an understandable expectation of experience to justify both the level of position and the salary.

An M.B.A. without any business experience would actually hurt your career because employers are unwilling to hire and pay for an M.B.A. degree without an accompanying high level of practical experience.

The job market is tough and is going to stay tough. For this reason, the M.B.A. beckons all those business graduates who feel that getting the degree will add something to their résumé and who hope the job market improves before they reenter it with the added credential of their new graduate degree. This is not a wise strategy because you continue to add unproven education without experience. Sadly, many of your peers who have taken M.B.A.s with no real-world experience will tell you their salaries and job descriptions are little different from those of another employee with a bachelor's degree.

This chapter is all about making your decision to get an M.B.A. a thoughtful choice, a choice that will not only enable you to get the most out of the degree, but also enhance your job prospects in the process.

Where Are You in This Picture?

First of all, consider one of the following scenarios to see if any fit your current thinking or situation:

Scenario 1: You've enjoyed your business major and done pretty well academically but you're not certain about exactly what kind of work you should look for. You're confused about what you can do in the workforce and who will hire you.

Scenario 2: You're approaching graduation or you've just graduated. You've tested the job market and it doesn't seem like a good time to be employed. Jobs are hard to come by, low paying, and don't seem to value your degree. Maybe you think it would be better to stay in school, get an advanced degree, and then try the job market.

Scenario 3: Perhaps you've done the kinds of job search activities suggested in the opening chapters of this book and seen all the better jobs and big money go to those who have an M.B.A.. You think, "OK, I'll get an M.B.A.," but you're worried about your own lack of work experience in a professional business environment. You wonder if you could get through the degree. You have to ask yourself if you have what it takes.

You may begin to feel as confused and frustrated as Shakespeare's Hamlet, wrestling over the question of whether or not to continue your education with an M.B.A. or to get out of school and go to work. Certainly, given the uncertainties of the job market and the shifting paradigms of employers and employee bases, it might seem a wise investment to continue to add to your business education, to earn an advanced degree, and hope to make yourself more competitive than the typical undergraduate job candidate.

Graduate school has always been a popular option, for those who could afford it, when the job market is tight. Enroll in business school, wait a couple of years, and then hopefully enter the market at a more propitious time. The strategy is that, hopefully, not only will your chances of employment be better, but once you have an advanced degree you may be a candidate for more and different jobs than you would have been previously and at a higher salary.

The Catch-22 of No Experience

Business school officials want students who have work experience; such pupils learn more and contribute more to a dynamic classroom environment. M.B.A. program curricula are built around adding to and enhancing the lessons with students' own personal experiences. When rising numbers of applicants for quality M.B.A. programs created enough admissions competition, discerning M.B.A. programs were able to require this work history for consideration for admission.

This work experience requirement obviously causes problems for the typical undergraduate applicant. For unless students without work experience are willing to enter lower-tier business schools that may have less demanding admissions requirements regarding work experience, they must somehow land excellent jobs rights from college. We all know those good jobs have been proven to be hard to attain without certain entry skills. The very top business students may qualify for employment at management consulting firms or financial institutions upon receipt of their bachelor's degree, but average students find they aren't competitive. What can you do?

Naturally, at this point, the clever student's intention turns to enhancing his or her attractiveness to an employer by getting an M.B.A.. But you cannot get into the top M.B.A. programs without first landing a good job. Since you intend your work experience to boost you into further schooling after a year or two on the job, you are in a weak position with a prospective employer.

Interestingly, this is where the experience catch causes problems, not just for students but for the colleges they've graduated from. The value of your undergraduate business program is weakened by the lower quality of the employment you finally do secure on your way to the M.B.A.. Your undergraduate program may not have been the boost to your job entry that you had hoped, nor does the degree appear to enhance your prospects for graduate school.

Let's identify some facts about M.B.A. programs and their students that might be important to you in weighing the advantages and disadvantages of making a graduate school choice without experience.

First, many M.B.A. students are older than the average new college graduate. The students in the 2001 graduating classes of that year's M.B.A. schools were, on average, twenty-nine years old, and those in the top thirty schools had 4.6 years of professional work experience, according to *Business Week* (*BW*, October 21, 2002) when they entered the program. More than 99 percent had some experience, and 93 percent had worked for more than two years.

Second, many M.B.A. students are in school because they need the degree to advance in their organizations. They may, in fact, be funded by their employers, and they are likely to approach their studies with the seriousness, responsibility, and expectation of superior performance that you would associate with someone there under the aegis of an employer. For these students, graduate work is "part of their job" and they approach it with the same gritty determination they would approach any work project. They are aggressive about their education, assertive with their classmates, less interested in the social aspects of graduate school, and more focused on their performance.

Third, another very unique aspect of the M.B.A. is the content of the course work, which centers around case studies—written stories of actual business practices. Individually or in teams, graduate students take these cases apart, analyze them, and prescribe real-world solutions. This is almost impossible to do when your own business experience is limited to the kinds of employment available to undergraduates during the summer or on school breaks.

Fourth, while your undergraduate grades may be superior and you may have already gained some solid work experience, including an internship in business, it's important to realize most business schools utilize the work group to accomplish many assignments and projects. Even if you are a superior student, if you have had limited group work in college, you may not be ready for the hard-driving, highly organized, and demanding group work of the experienced businesspeople in your classes. That is a skill often learned on the job, and you may find it hard to deal with the candid feedback on your performance by group members in addition to appraisals used by course instructors.

Finally, students who have a work history enter the graduate business school with a focus, be it sales, management, finance, real estate, law, or production. This focus enables them to target courses and focus their attention on the most relevant and useful material in the program. This is not apt to occur without the relevant work experience.

Gaining Admission to B-School

For the candidate who approaches the admission office of a graduate business school, two elements of the application can be particularly important: a strong personal essay and an interview (even if not required). Both are good indicators of your readiness for an M.B.A. program. With each, admissions committees will be looking for maturity, drive, and focus. The personal essay required by your application should clearly enunciate your:

- Motivation
- Goals
- Degree of readiness

An excellent guide to writing this essay is *How to Write a Winning Personal Statement for Graduate and Professional School,* by Richard J. Stelzer (Princeton, NJ: Petersons Guides, 1997). Examining these issues in preparation for such a personal essay is a valuable experience in and of itself and may shed some light on the question, "To M.B.A. or not?" Further information on the application process can be found in *How to Get into the Right Business School* by James L. Strachan (Lincolnwood: VGM Career Books, 1999).

If it is at all possible, even when not required, try to have a personal interview at the school. The interview will allow the school to question you and probe for the elements listed above, and it will provide an opportunity for you to explain your decision to seek an M.B.A. and to discuss your commitment to the world of business.

A Suggested Career Path to the M.B.A.

An ideal job for the business school undergraduate contemplating graduate school would be a position of some sophistication, reasonable salary, and yet, no expectation that you would stay there for very long. In fact, what would be even more ideal would be a position where the expectation was that you would leave (even have to leave) to return to graduate school. Such positions do exist. Typical position titles are research analyst or research associate (RA) in management consulting firms, and financial analyst (FA) at investment banks or investment banking departments of commercial banks. They may also be called business analysts, associate consultants, or just associates. The essential thing is that they all perform similar roles.

Most of these positions are in business consulting firms. These firms provide advice and services to other businesses, which become their clients. Some of these client businesses need help; they're in trouble over product development, staffing issues, profit and loss projections, or any of a host of complicated situations. Others are doing well and need assistance to cope with rapid growth; still others need help increasing profitability or efficiency. Consulting can be utilized by any business for any aspect of a business's operation. If you like business, you should enjoy consulting.

Job Duties

Generally, you will be doing library research, collecting data in organized forms, and conducting some data manipulations. Research associates or financial analysts assist in helping to put together proposals, case studies, or analyses designed to help the consultant's client solve problems, determine future strategies, or implement programs. As you gain expertise, some responsibilities will be added, in most cases having to do with additional and more sophisticated research capabilities, quantitative manipulation of data using computer software, and the presentation of findings to your work team.

There is a limit on what you can do, on the decisions you will be allowed to make, and in how far you can go on your own. These positions have been structured for rapid turnover and for people to work under more senior positions who have those decision-making responsibilities.

Because these positions are designed to appeal to graduates contemplating advanced education, they are not designed to fulfill career aspirations. Though they come with a salary and benefits, they have more in common with internships than typical entry-level positions. In fact, these analyst positions are often part of special hiring programs. Since the job only lasts for two years, many entry-level candidates are recruited and hired, and the training and mentoring involved for the new analysts is considerable. The responsibilities are located in one individual or office that manages the research associate/analyst program. The defined boundaries of the experience and the structure of the internal training process should be highly acceptable to the bachelor's degree student seeking to gain valuable skills and experience before entering graduate school.

Strategic Advantages

Job candidates applying for these positions do not have to misrepresent their intentions of leaving for an M.B.A.. In fact, if you should desire to stay, you would find upon investigation that senior responsibility and authority is reserved for those with the M.B.A., so you would have to get an M.B.A. anyway.

Many analysts do, in fact, return to the consulting firms and banks that initially hired them after obtaining their M.B.A. At this point, they begin new career paths in positions with complicated titles such as "associate-to-consultant." (Some of the top firms have the luxury of hiring only M.B.A.s, even for associate positions.) These titles recognize they are on their way to the coveted consulting partnerships in the organization.

Whatever your choice upon coming to the close of your two years as a research associate, you are in a very different position than when you graduated from college. You have significant, important business experience that will have transformed the value of your undergraduate degree. You are well situated to apply to one of the top graduate business programs and feel confident about your ability to succeed.

Whatever graduate program you do enter, you arrive better prepared to make the most of the degree. When you graduate with your M.B.A., you offer your new employer excellent justification for a responsible, decision-making position with all the appropriate rewards of such a job.

Perhaps in reading through this strategy, you've begun to have some doubts about its suitability in your case. Though you agree with the proposition, you don't feel like the ideal candidate. Your objections might be on any number of grounds: your grades in college may not have been good enough for you to be competitive for some of these consulting positions; or maybe your objection is you are not interested in resettling for any amount of time in the urban areas occupied by this type of business; or it may be that the nature of the work of research associates as described does not interest you. You still have options.

The basic premise of this book has been to suggest the importance of acquiring portable skills; that is, skills that you can carry from job to job. Content skills are pertinent to one job and not easily transferable to another. Portable skills follow you throughout your career. In today's and tomorrow's ever-changing job market, portable skills offer you the best measure of job security.

Suggesting the research analyst path before you get an M.B.A. accomplishes two things: you gain those important portable skills from the job itself, and you guarantee success in the M.B.A. program and after you graduate.

But if, for the reasons listed above or perhaps other reasons, this path to the M.B.A. isn't for you, you can still accomplish the same goals in a slightly different way by seeking out positions after graduation that provide the same kind of preparation as the consulting firms do, but without the same intensity of competition or the geographic restrictions or the job task definitions.

These are, of course, career positions and not the two-year, self-liquidating kinds of positions described in the career path. You will need to honestly negotiate and express your intentions about advanced education and work out a solution with your employers to ensure that, if you do decide to leave for graduate school, you leave with excellent recommendations and the possibility to return. You may decide to go to graduate school at night and hold on to your position. In fact, the employer may offer you educational benefits as an inducement to that course of action. And, of course, you may find your job so interesting, with so many possibilities for personal enrichment, that you decide not to go to graduate school, at least for the foreseeable future. Whatever your decision, you will have begun to build upon your undergraduate education with valuable work experience that benefits both your career and any possibility of future professional education.

Working Conditions

If you are working for a consulting firm of the size that can afford a number of research or financial associates or an investment bank or investment department of a commercial bank large enough to have such a department, you should be thinking in terms of a major metropolitan area or the highway belt around such an area. This is where you will find the concentration of employers hosting these kinds of positions.

As a career counselor, I have discovered there are a variety of reactions to living in a metropolitan area—some people love the idea and others don't. Most will admit, however, that metropolitan living offers more choices than any other locale, more choices in living, more choices about shopping, more choices in entertainment, and many more opportunities to meet people.

It's good to note that many fine graduate schools of business are also located in these major population zones, and that may prove convenient when it comes time to move ahead in your strategic plan to enter an M.B.A. program.

There is no typical day for a research associate or financial analyst in consulting or investment banking. However, while there may be no daily routines (and that in itself may be an attraction for you), the following activities and roles played are fairly constant over time.

Information Resourcing

These associate positions all require finding answers, usually under pressure of time and cost. To succeed, you need to be inventive, to be good on the phone, and to believe you can do it. In most consulting and investment decisions, information needs to be of high quality and recent. Providing that information will be a big part of your daily job. Your day will probably begin by scanning several newspapers, watching for business and market information that might prove helpful. Begin that newspaper reading practice now. It'll come in very handy in your M.B.A. program.

Financial analyst positions at investment banks or in the investment department of larger banks monitor the performance of particular stocks and securities on the world's stock exchanges and stay well informed about the industries they track. Generally, you will focus on one or two industries in this kind of position.

Travel

Long-distance travel is more a function of the research associate in the consulting industry than the analyst in investment banking. Some entry-level consulting positions can involve a grueling amount of travel. Just as the problems are global, clients can be global as well. Consultants leave the United States every day for China, Latin America, and Eastern Europe. Many of our largest consulting firms and investment banking services have had a strong European presence for decades. This increasingly far-flung demand for consulting/analyst services gives an edge to the individual with language skills and/or cultural sensitivity. Both research and financial analyst positions can involve significant out-of-the-office time in meetings with and working on-site with clients. To succeed, you need to be flexible and willing to get up and go. When you are on-site with the client, there tend to be correspondingly long days, because your client knows you aren't going home, but to a hotel.

Analysis

Designing or running complicated computer models to evaluate corporations or monitor stock price movement, or daily work with numerous databases to retrieve important information will consume much of your time. You will need to become familiar with all kinds of statistical digests, annual reports, Securities and Exchange Commission documents, spreadsheets, and financial market reports.

Whether you need to analyze the investment potential of a foreign firm, the comparable company activity pursuant to a merger, or the involved preparations prior to a public offering of stock, you will encounter data that needs to be transformed into usable information by your analysis. This information will then become the basis for the consulting team's action plan for the client.

This manipulation and understanding of data will provide some of the most valuable experience you can bring to your M.B.A. program. It is perhaps one of the most crucial skills for graduate work; and your ability to transform "data" into "information" should help to make your journey through the M.B.A. program a smooth one. You will have an advantage over many of your peers, even those with business experience, because as a consulting associate or financial analyst you are working for so many different clients on so many different projects that you will develop a broad understanding of resources and relevant techniques.

Presentation

In a consulting firm, the work is underwritten by client fees. Though you may be working on several different projects simultaneously, all your work is client directed and available to the client for examination and review. Attractive presentation of materials is a skill you will begin to appreciate in consulting. The presentation may be a carefully prepared written document with charts and graphs (demanding mastery of software products) or it may be a public presentation with overheads, handouts, and your explanations of your material as well as responses to questions. Creativity, quality work with deadlines, and skills with a variety of presentation techniques are what you will take away from this experience. This will be valuable in your M.B.A. program and later in your career.

Teamwork

As a research associate or analyst, all of your work supports more senior staff people who have the major responsibility for the success or failure of a client contract. Consequently, a team approach is important in everything you'll do. You'll learn to clearly communicate your activities to your team members in order to avoid overlaps, misunderstandings, and wasted effort on anyone's part. This team approach will stand you in good stead in your M.B.A. program.

Training and Qualifications

Let's begin with a rather general statement of training for RAs and FAs from the *Occupational Outlook Handbook* for 2002–2003, published by the U.S. Department of Labor, Bureau of Labor Statistics (BLS).

There are no universal educational requirements for entry-level jobs in this field. However, employers in private industry prefer to hire those with a master's degree in business administration or a discipline related to the firm's area of specialization. Those individuals hired straight out of school with only a bachelor's degree are likely to work as research associates or junior consultants, rather than full-fledged management consultants. It is possible for research associates to advance up the career ladder if they demonstrate a strong aptitude for consulting, but, more often, they need to get an advanced degree to do so.

Employers of these positions will be looking for people with some very specific qualifications. Strong candidates will possess very strong quantitative, analytical, and communications skills. They will be able to work in fast-paced, demanding environments, and they will need to demonstrate achievements such as a high GPA, sophisticated academic and part-time work experience, and extracurricular leadership positions.

Consulting is done in a wide variety of contexts by some of the most prestigious firms in the world. While most consulting falls under the rubric of management consulting, there is a diverse set of other areas where consulting is provided. Broadly speaking, the job requirements are as follows:

- People skills: high
- Sales skills: medium
- Communication skills: high
- Analytical skills: extremely high
- Ability to synthesize: high
- Creative ability: high
- Initiative: medium
- Computer skills: medium
- Work hours: 50–90/week

Earnings

Starting salaries in consulting positions (analyst position) with a bachelor's degree, after bonus, range from $30,000 to $50,000. Starting salaries with an M.B.A. degree (associate position) range, after bonus, from $40,000 to $125,000. These salaries vary with firms and with the region of the country you are in. The Bureau of Labor Statistics looked at a broader category of management analysts, which included management consultants, in 2000, and came up with an average salary of $60,000, with the top 10 percent earning $98,000-plus. What you need to remember in reading these very generous salary figures is that these firms have their employees under tremendous scrutiny. If you don't perform, you'll be let go. This remains true even as you climb the salary ladder. Many of these firms have very specific expectations for when employees should be achieving certain levels of performance. When you see high earnings such as these, you shouldn't be surprised that the following are true: (1) getting hired will be correspondingly difficult, and (2) you will work very hard, indeed, for that salary.

U.S. News and World Report reported the following median salaries in consulting in the mid-1990s:

Research associate	$30,400
Entry-level consultant	$41,800
Management consultant	$89,200
Senior consultant	$120,100
Junior partner	$120,100
Senior partner	$194,000

An informal survey of new employees in various consulting firms showed dramatic variability in salaries.

Career Outlook

The consulting industry has really been growing in the last few years. Two outcomes of that growth have been: (1) companies today are more likely to "buy" from among this growing array of specific consulting services to solve problems, rather than hire permanent staff to accomplish the same things, and (2) firms who hire associates on these two-year programs find the turnover keeps their permanent staff vital, energetic, and competitive.

Add to that list the volatile business environment in the 1990s and 2000s that has challenged even smaller corporations with issues of global competition, dramatic technological advances, and an endless stream of new thinking and practices for organizational structure. Faced with this kind of dizzying environment, it's no wonder management cries, "Get us a consultant!"

One interesting point of fact is that industry analysts have tracked the consulting industry, which grew by leaps and bounds through the 1990s. Hiring is and will continue to be an active process, and strong demand is anticipated to continue. The Census of Business found 64,657 U.S. management consulting services firms with annual payrolls of $32 billion in 1999.

Strategy for Finding the Jobs

If you've decided you want to enter an M.B.A. program after first taking a position as a financial analyst or research associate, you're already further ahead in finding one of those jobs than you think! Why? Just as you've made a decision to seek an M.B.A. at some point in your future by first acquiring some valuable portable skills, potential employers have determined that they want employees who have direction and goals in their lives. You will be setting yourself apart from countless other graduates with your ability to articulate your life plan and future aspirations. Even if the individuals talking with you don't entirely agree with the specific details of your decisions, they will respect the thinking and planning that you've done and realize it sets you apart from your contemporaries.

If you want a consulting position, don't start by looking through the "Help Wanted" section of your paper. Consulting firms do not advertise or publish entry-level research associate or financial analyst positions. Why not? These are highly selective positions and there are limited numbers of them. Furthermore, consulting firms and investment banking organizations assume that one indication of candidates' suitability for this kind of role will be their ability to seek these positions out on their own.

The following is an extensive listing of consulting firms that will facilitate a good beginning to your search activities. Additionally, the articles cited are a selection from recent periodical literature focusing on consulting. They will give you a good sense of what's happening in the industry. They will also give you additional names of potential employers and provide you with an excellent basis for an in-depth interview with these kinds of employers! Finally, the list of directories will lead you to hundreds of other possible employers of various types and sizes.

Leading Firms in Management Consulting

Accenture
161 N. Clark St.
Chicago, IL 60601
(312) 693-0161
2001 revenues: $11.4 billion. Clients: Boston Scientific, Alcatel, Simon & Schuster, Daimler-Chrysler.

A. T. Kearney
222 West Adams St.
Chicago, IL 60606
(312) 648-0111

2001 revenues: $1.33 billion. Number of consultants: 2,800. Recent clients: GM, Sears, Gillette, France Telecom, Unilever, Deutsche Bank, Mitsubishi Corp., BP, FedEx. Note: A. T. Kearney is a subsidiary of EDS.

Booz Allen Hamilton
8283 Greensboro Dr.
McLean, VA, 22102
2002 revenues: $2.1 billion. Number of consultants: 9,500. Recent clients: Internal Revenue Service, Nissan Motor Company, BP Amoco, National Security Agency.

Computer Sciences Corporation (CSC)
2100 E. Grand Ave.
El Segundo, CA 90245
(310) 615-0311
csc.com
2002 revenues: $11.4 billion. Number of employees: 67,000 worldwide. Clients: U.S. Postal Service, E-Plus (Germany), DuPont, AT&T, United Technologies, Nortel, Gulfstream Aerospace, U.S. Air Force

IBM Business Consulting Services
11 Madison Ave.
New York, NY 10010
(646) 471-4000
ibm.com/services
2001 revenues (global gross): $7.5 billion. Number of employees: 32,000; offices in fifty-two countries. Clients in 2001: nearly half of the Fortune Global 500 were represented and 82 percent of the European Financial Times 50.

Mercer Management Consulting, Inc.
1166 Avenue of the Americas
New York, NY 10036
(212) 345-8000
Fax: (212) 345-8075
Send career inquiries to:
Recruiting Office
Mercer Management Consulting
33 Hayden Ave.
Lexington, MA 02421

2001 revenues: $2.2 billion. Mercer Management Consulting is part of the Mercer Consulting Group. Number of professionals: 1,100 in twenty-one offices worldwide. Recent clients: Philips, United Airlines, Deutsche Telekom.

The Monitor Group
2 Canal Park
Cambridge, MA 02141
(617) 252-2000
2000 revenues: $300 million. Number of consultants: 1,000. Offices: twenty-nine in twenty-five countries. Clients: Leading Fortune 500 companies in the United States, *Financial Times* 100 index and leading companies in many other countries.

Selected Books and Articles

"Consulting Careers Reach New Heights in Popularity," *Business Credit*, January 1999 (National Association of Credit Management).

"The Craze for Consultants: How Management Can Get Its Money's Worth," *Business Week*, July 25, 1994, pp. 60–66.

"The Ever-Bigger Boom in Consulting," *Fortune*, April 24, 1989, p. 113.

How to Make It Big as a Consultant, by William A Cohen (New York: Amacom, 2001).

"Let's Go for Growth," *Fortune*, March 7, 1994, p. 60. Describes a popular 1990s business strategy: high growth. Good background reading for an interview in consulting.

"Lock the Doors. It's EDS." *Business Week*, September 19, 1994, p. 36. Describes the aggressive strategy of EDS in the management consulting business.

"The McKinsey Mystique," *Business Week*, September 20, 1993, p. 66. Describes the workings of top-of-the-line McKinsey & Co. ("The Firm") and close relations with corporate America.

"The Selling of a B-School Grad," *Business Week*, March 28, 1994, p. 146.

Other Resources Including Directories

The Career Guide: Dun's Employment Opportunities Directory (Parsippany, NJ: Dun's Marketing Services).

This gives an alphabetic listing of corporations and investment banks explaining career opportunities, personnel requirements, training and career development practices, benefits, and addresses.

Consultants and Consulting Organizations Directory 22nd ed. (Detroit, MI: Gale Research, 2000).
This comprehensive directory lists over 20,000 businesses and individuals who consult for businesses and government.

Consultants News
Kennedy Publications
Templeton Road
Fitzwilliam, NH 03447
Available from the Consultants Bookstore at (603) 585-2200. This publication covers the industry of management consulting, covering recent trends and who is growing.

Directory of Management Consultants
Kennedy Publications
Templeton Road
Fitzwilliam, NH 03447
Available from the Consultants Bookstore at (603) 585-2200. This excellent directory lists consultants of all kinds and gives specialties, locations, and phone numbers.

Harvard Business School Career Guide: Management Consulting (Boston: Harvard Business School Press, 1994).
Lists job descriptions in leading consulting firms including contact persons for M.B.A. students and phone numbers. An invaluable resource. (617) 495-6700.

Nelson's Directory of Investment Research. (Port Chester, NY: Nelson Publications, 1995).
A superior source of firms that hire investment analyst type positions: investment banks, investment departments, and brokerage houses.

Consulting Firms

There's no question that breaking into the top firms like Bain, McKinsey, and Mercer will be a challenge. These firms target top schools and hire heavily from this pool. On the other hand, some superb second-tier firms have hired thousands of consultants on college campuses and are regular recruiters at the top job fairs as well.

Looking for employers in the fields of investment banking and consulting requires a resource that gives you a "big picture" look at industries. One of the best is a book by Leila K. Kight, *Getting the Lowdown on Employers and a Leg Up on the Job Market* (Berkeley, CA: Ten Speed Press, 1994). It will help you do basic research on industries, employers, and government agencies. Kight teaches you valuable techniques to use other research sources wisely, too.

Many consulting firms specialize in specific kinds of consulting or have specific areas of expertise in the field. Below are some examples of this, along with the names of firms utilizing that approach.

Strategic Consulting. These consultants help with strategic planning for the subsequent two to five years. Consultation might include choosing a strategy for growth, making suggestions for restructuring, providing international expertise, suggesting acquisitions or divestitures, and/or revitalizing leadership. While not applying fixed "recipes," some consulting firms are known for having a specific perspective. Gemini Consulting, for example, suggests that businesses transform themselves using the "four Rs": reframing corporate issues, restructuring the company, revitalizing, and then renewing the organization and its people. Prominent firms in strategic consulting include:

A. T. Kearney (Chicago, Illinois)
Accenture (Chicago, Illinois)
Bain & Co. (Boston, Massachusetts)
Booz Allen Hamilton (New York City)
Boston Consulting Group (Boston, Massachusetts)
Cap Gemini Ernst & Young   (Morristown, New Jersey)
IBM Consulting/PWC (New York City)
McKinsey & Co. (New York City)
Mercer Management Consulting (New York City)
Monitor (Cambridge, Massachusetts)

Business Process Reengineering Consulting. An important trend in business in the last five years is the enormous push to increase productivity through improving business processes. Business process reanalysis and design has been important to the following firms:

Boston Consulting Group (Boston)
CSC Consulting (Cambridge, MA)
IBM Consulting/PWC (New York)

Systems Consulting. Consultants provide firms with services that involve specialized knowledge, a fresh perspective, and a high level of expertise. It would be hard to find an area that fits this description better than that of systems consulting. These consultants offer advice to organizations about the optimal configuration of their information systems, the integration of their information systems, the introduction of client-server computing, and the purchase of hardware and software. Prominent players in this market include:

Cap Gemini Ernst & Young (Morristown, New Jersey)
CSC Index (Cambridge, Massachusetts)
Digital Consulting (Maynard, Massachusetts)
EDS (Plano, Texas)
Cap Gemini Ernst & Young (Morristown, New Jersey)
IBM Consulting/PWC (Armonk, New York)
Technology Solutions (Chicago, Illinois)

Human Resources Consulting. Some of the most important and sensitive decisions in any firms involve who to hire, how to compensate and motivate them, and how to develop their skills. Human resource consultants offer advice on such things as compensation and benefits packages, pension funds, benefits of a diverse workforce, and employee development programs. Some leading human resource consultants are:

Automated Concepts (Chicago, Illinois)
Hewitt Associates (Lincolnshire, Illinois)
Towers Perrin (Chicago, Illinois)
Watson Wyatt Group (Chicago, Illinois)

Litigation Consulting. The complexity of litigation has increased significantly in recent decades. As a result, the demand by law firms for litigation support has risen dramatically. Litigation consultants provide this support by working with attorneys to map out case strategies, develop courtroom exhibits and tactics, and provide economic analysis of the advantages or disadvantages of litigation. This position requires good analytical and problem-solving skills. Some of the many firms in this business include:

Charles River Associates (Boston, Massachusetts)
Cornerstone Research (Menlo Park, California)
Economic Analysis Corporation (Los Angeles, California)
FinEcon (Los Angeles, California)
Law & Economics Consulting Group (Emeryville, California)
Litigation Sciences (Los Angeles, California)

Micronomics (Los Angeles, California)
National Economic Research Associates (White Plains, New York)
Price Waterhouse (Los Angeles and New York City)

Finance Consulting. Financial consultants provide financial advice to corporations and money managers. This advice may involve pricing of securities, strategies for creating shareholder value, business valuation, economic forecasts and analysis, and/or suggestions for treasury management. Firms involved in this growing area include:

A. B. Laffer & Associates (Los Angeles, California)
Alcar Group (Chicago, Illinois)
Andrew Kalotay Associates (Sea Cliff, New York)
Boston Consulting Group (Boston, Massachusetts)
Houlihan Lokey Howard & Zukin (Los Angeles, California)
Ibbotson Associates (Chicago, Illinois)
McKinsey & Co. (New York City)
Stanford Consulting Group (Menlo Park, California)
Stern Stewart & Co. (New York City)
Wilshire Associates (Los Angeles, California)

Beyond Business School

If you do decide to pursue the idea of two years of professional experience before business graduate school, either with a consulting firm or some alternative choice of your own devising, one obvious place to turn once you've achieved that graduate business degree is back to your original employer.

And that does happen frequently. Generally, the work, the compensation, and the level of management expertise is worthy of your commitment and your advanced education. The very qualities that drew you to these experiences as solid preparation for your M.B.A. are still valid for your work post-M.B.A.

One word of caution here. If you do return to your original employer after graduate school, you'll find things have, naturally, changed. At the same time, you, too, are no longer the same job candidate. You're older, you're wiser, and you have expectations of a position and responsibilities both commensurate with your new degree and built upon your previous experience. It will be your job to point out that you are no longer the same job candidate. If, during the interview process, you determine you are still being viewed as the trainee you were before, you might do better to look elsewhere and start with a fresh slate.

With an M.B.A. and solid work experience in a consulting firm or investment banking organization, before and/or after securing your graduate degree, there is always the temptation to consider going solo as a consultant.

An enhancement to the solo consultant is attaining the designation of Certified Management Consultant (CMC). For information on achieving this designation, contact:

Institute of Management Consultants
230 Park Ave., Suite 544
New York, NY 10169

As your career progresses, another important consideration for going solo is keeping up a good network of contacts. In your work as an associate with a consulting firm or as a financial analyst in an investment bank and even during your M.B.A., you will become acquainted with numerous other talented individuals who will rise in their respective businesses, and it is important to stay in touch with them. They may be future customers.

Professional Associations

Professional associations remain the hidden treasure for job seekers. These organizations have a vested interest in raising the general information level of recent graduates about the career fields they represent. Most are very generous with their publications and providing answers to questions. Give them a try.

American Association of Healthcare Consultants
1926 Waukegan Rd.
Glenview, IL 60025
(847) 657-6964
aahc.net
Members/Purpose: Serves as a resource for health-care providers; offers continuing education to members. Provides information concerning the role of hospital/health consultants
Publication: Membership directory.

American Association of Political Consultants
600 Pennsylvania Ave. SE, Suite 330
Washington, DC 20003
(202) 544-9315

Members/Purpose: Regular members are corporations and individuals who devote a major portion of their livelihood to political counseling and related activities. The association provides a vehicle for the exchange of information, resources, and ideas among its members.
Publications: Membership roster, newsletter.

American Association of
Professional Consultants
(AAPC)
Management Consulting Center
1850 Fifth Ave.
San Diego, CA 92101
(619) 239-7076
Fax: (619) 296-3580
nationalbureau@att.net
national-bureau.com
Members/Purpose: Professional consultants. Aids and guides members in the improvement of their professional abilities.
Publications: *The Consultant's Journal, The Consultant's Voice*, membership directory.

American Consultants League
30466 Prince William St.
Princess Anne, MD 21853
(410) 651-4869
consultantsinstitute.com
Members/Purpose: Full- and part-time consultants in varied fields of expertise. Provides assistance to consultants in establishing and managing the business component of their consultancies.
Publications: *Consultants Directory, Consulting Intelligence, How to Mass Market Your Advice, The Consultants Malpractice Avoidance Manual.*

American Society of
Agricultural Consultants
950 S. Cherry St., Suite 508
Denver, CO 80246-2664
agconsultants.com
Members/Purpose: Strives to maintain high standards of ethics and competence in the consulting field.
Publication: Newsletter.

Association of Managing Consultants
521 Fifth Ave., 35th Floor
New York, NY 10175
Members/Purpose: Professional management consulting firms who serve
all types of business and industry.
Training: Sponsors specialized education dealing with professional
development.
Publications: *Directory of Membership, Journal of Management Consulting*,
newsletter.

Association of Master Business
Administration Executives (AMBAE)
AMBA Center
227 Commerce St.
East Haven, CT 06512
Members/Purpose: Private corporation of master of business
administration executives to serve their professional career and financial
needs.
Training: Conducts seminars.
Publications: *AMBA Network*, newsletter, *MBA Employment Guide*
(semiannual), *MBA Industry Reports*.

Council of Consulting Organizations
521 Fifth Ave., 35th Floor
New York, NY 10175
Members/Purpose: Individual management consultants who work privately
or in consulting firms that meet the institute's requirements.
Publication: *Directory of Members*.

Independent Computer Consultants
Association
11131 South Towne Square, Suite F
St. Louis, MO 63123
Members/Purpose: Promotes professionalism within the industry;
increased awareness in the general business community of the products
and services available; and provides members with group benefits.
Training: Conducts educational programs.
Publications: *The Independent, Tax*, and *Handbook for Consultants and
Clients*.

Institute of Management Consultants
2025 M St.
Washington, DC 20036-3309
(202) 367-1134
imcusa.org
Members/Purpose: Organization of consultants has local chapters in many
cities. The institute's mission is one of education and certification of
consultants to encourage excellence and ethics in the profession.

MBA/Business Executives: American Management Association
130 West Fiftieth St.
New York, NY 10020
Members/Purpose: Seeks to broaden members' management knowledge
and skills.
Training: Conducts the Extension Institute, a private self-paced study
program, and Operation Enterprise, a young adult program for high
school/college level students. Offers courses, workshops, and briefings.
Publications: *Compensation and Benefits Review, Compflash, Management
Review, Organizational Dynamics, The President, Project Update,
Supervisory Management, Management Solutions, Supervisory Sense,* and
Trainers Workshop.

Society of Professional Business Consultants
621 Plainfield Rd., No. 308
Willowbrook, IL 60521
Members/Purpose: Persons engaged in rendering business consultant
services to physicians and dentists. Provides members with educational
information to upgrade their effectiveness as professionals.
Publications: *The Consultant,* newsletter, roster.

Additional Resources

ABI/Inform (CD-Rom) (Ann Arbor, MI: Proquest Information and Learning Annual/Periodic Update).

AHA Guide to the Health Care Field (Chicago: American Hospital Association, annual).

America's Corporate Families, 2 vols. (Bethlehem, PA: Dun & Bradstreet Information Services, 1996).

America's Top Internet Job Sites: Finding a Job Online by Ron and Caryl Krannich (Manassas Park, VA: Impact Publications, 2001).

America's Top Medical and Human Services Jobs (Indianapolis: JIST Publishing, 2000).

American Salaries and Wages Survey, 6th ed. (Detroit: Gale Group, 2001).

AV Market Place 2002 (New Providence, NJ: R. R. Bowker, annual).

The Best Companies for Minorities by Lawrence Graham (New York: Plume Books, 1993).

Best's Insurance Reports (Oldwick, NJ: A. M. Best Co., semiannual serials since 1985).

Black's Medical Dictionary (New York: Madison Books, 1999).

Burrelle's Media Directory 2002 (Livingston, NJ: Burrelle's Media Directories, 2002).

Business Rankings Annual 2003 (Detroit: Gale Group, annual).

Career Alternatives for Bankers by William B. King (Nashville: Magellan Press, 1998).

The Career Guide: Dun's Employment Opportunities Directory (Bethlehem, PA: Dun & Bradstreet Information Services, 1997).

Career Information Center, 8th ed. (Detroit: Gale Group/Macmillan Library Reference, 2001).

Career Opportunities in Banking Finance and Insurance by Thomas P. Fitch (New York: Facts on File, 2002).

Careers in Healthcare by Barbara Swanson (Chicago: VGM Career Books, 2000).

Careerjournal.com (website)
Dow Jones & Co., Inc.
New York, NY

Careers Encyclopedia (Chicago: VGM Career Books, 1997).
Careers in Advertising (Chicago: VGM Career Books, 1996).
Careers in Business (Chicago: VGM Career Books, 1998).
Careers in Communications (Chicago: VGM Career Books, 1998).
Careers in Computers (Chicago: VGM Career Books, 2002).
Careers in Finance (Chicago: VGM Career Books, 1999).
Careers in Government (Chicago: VGM Career Books, 1999).
Careers in Health Care (Chicago: VGM Career Books, 2000).
Careers in High Tech (Chicago: VGM Career Books, 1998).
Careers in Social and Rehabilitation Services (Chicago: VGM Career Books, 2001).
Carroll's State Directory: Executive, Legislative, Judicial (Washington, DC: Carroll Publishing Co., 2002).
The Chronicle of Higher Education (Lancaster, PA: Editorial Projects for Education, serial publication starting 1966).
The College Board Guide to Jobs and Career Planning by Joyce S. Mitchell (New York: The College Board, 1994). collegeboard.com.
Community Jobs: The National Employment Newspaper for the Non-Profit Sector (ACCESS: Networking in the Public Interest) (Boston: Community Careers Resource Center, monthly serial).
The Complete Guide to Public Employment, 3rd ed., by Ronald Krannich and Caryl Krannich (Woodbridge, VA: Impact Publications, 1994).
Consultants and Consulting Organizations Directory, 22nd ed. (Detroit, MI: Gale Group, 2000).
Consultants News (Petersborough, NH: Kennedy Publications, monthly serial). kennedyinfo.com.
Current Jobs in Writing, Editing and Communications (Washington, DC: Plymouth Publishing, Inc., monthly serial).
Developing a Lifelong Contract in the Sports Marketplace, 4th ed., by Greg Cylkowski (Little Canada, MN: Athletic Achievements, 1998).

Dialing for Jobs (video) (Indianapolis: JIST Publishing, 2002).

Dictionary of Holland Occupational Codes, 3rd ed. (Odessa, FL: Psychological Assessment Resources, 1996).

Dictionary of Occupational Titles (Washington, DC: U.S. Department of Labor Employment and Training Administration, 1992).

Dictionary of Occupational Titles, The O*Net (Indianapolis: JIST Works, 1998).

Directory of American Firms Operating in Foreign Countries, 16th ed. (New York: World Trade Academy Press, 2001).

Directory of American Research and Technology, 32nd ed. (New Providence, NJ: Reed Reference Publishing, 1998).

Directory of Bond Agents (East Rutherford, NJ: First Data Services, 2001 edition and later). (Pre-2001 editions published by Standard and Poor's Corp.)

Directory of Corporate Affiliations (Albany: LexisNexis, 2002).

Directory of Management Consultants (Peterborough, NH: Kennedy Information, Inc., 1977).

Directory of National Environmental Organizations (St. Paul, MN: U.S. Environmental Directories, 1994).

Dun's Consultants Directory (Bethlehem, PA: Dun & Bradstreet Information Services 1999).

Effective Answers to Interview Questions (video) (Indianapolis: JIST Publishing, 1992).

Encyclopedia of Associations (Detroit: Gale Group, 1999).

Encyclopedia of Business Information Sources (Detroit: Gale Group, 2000).

Encyclopedia of Medical Organizations and Agencies (Detroit: Gale Group, 2002)

The End of Work: The Decline of the Global Labor Force and the Dawn of the Post-Market Era by Jeremy Rifkin (New York: G.P. Putnam's Sons, 1995).

Environmental Industries Marketplace (Detroit: Gale Group, 1992).

Federal Career Opportunities (New York: Gordon Press Publishers, biweekly publication since 1980).

Federal Jobs Digest (Osinning, NY: Breakthrough Publications, biweekly journal). jobsfed.com

Federal Times (newspaper)
6883 Commercial Dr.
Springfield, VA 22159
federaltimes.com

Fedworld (website)
U.S. Department of Commerce
Springfield, VA
fedworld.gov

Flying High in Travel: A Complete Guide to Careers in the Travel Industry by Karen Rubin (New York: John Wiley & Sons, 1992).
Folio: The Magazine for Magazine Management (Stamford, CT).
Foreign Consular Offices in the United States (Washington, DC: U.S. Department of State, 2000).
Foundation Grants to Individuals (New York: The Foundation Center, 2002).
Gale Directory of Publications and Broadcast Media (Detroit: Gale Group, 2002).
Good Works: A Guide to Careers in Social Change edited by Donna Colvin (New York: Barricade Books, 1994).
Government Job Finder by Daniel Lauber (River Forest, IL: Planning/Communications, 1994).

Graduate Management Admissions Test Information
Graduate Management Admission Council
McLean, VA

Graduate Record Exam Information
Graduate Record Examinations Board
Educational Testing Service
Princeton, NJ

Great Careers: The Fourth of July Guide to Careers, Internships, and Volunteer Opportunities in the Nonprofit Sector by Devon Cottrell Smith (Garrett Park, MD: Garrett Park Press, 1990).
Green at Work by Susan Cohn (Washington, DC: Island Press, 1995).
Guide to America's Federal Jobs (Indianapolis: JIST Publishing, 2002).
Handbook for Business and Management Careers (Chicago: McGraw-Hill Professional, 1990).
Harrington-O'Shea Career Decision Making System (Circle Pines, MN: American Guidance Service, 1985).
Harvard Business School Career Guide: Management Consulting by Neil Nunn (Cambridge, MA: Harvard Business School Press, 1999).
Harvard Gazette (Cambridge, MA: Harvard Office of News & Public Affairs, weekly publication).

Health Care Job Explosion! by Dennis V. Damp (Coraopolis, PA: D-Amp Publications, 2001).

Healthcare Career Directory (Detroit: Gale Group, 1991).

Hoover's Handbook of American Business 2003—Profiles of 750 U.S. Corporations (Austin, TX: Hoover's Inc., 2003).

Hospital Market Atlas (Chicago: SMG Marketing Group, Inc., annual).

Index of Majors and Graduate Degrees 2003 (annual) (Forrester Center, WV: College Board Publications, 2003).

Infotrac CD-ROM General Businessfile ASAP (Foster City, CA: Information Access Co., 2002).

InternAmerica (bimonthly periodical)
The Internship Newsletter and News Service
105 Chestnut St., Suite 34
Needham, MA 02192

International Television Association Membership Directory (Irving, TX: International Television Association).

Internships 2003 (Princeton, NJ: Peterson's Guides, 2003).

Job Bank series (Holbrook, MA: Adams Media, Inc.).

Job Hotlines USA by Steven Wood (Harleyville, PA: Career Communications, Inc., 1994).

The Job Hunter: The National Bi-Weekly Publication for Job Seekers
Career Planning and Placement Center
University of Missouri–Columbia
100 Noyes Building
Columbia, MO 65211

Job Opportunities in Business (Princeton, NJ: Peterson's, 1999).

Job Opportunities: Health and Science (Princeton, NJ: Peterson's, 1999).

The Job Search Handbook for Educators: ASCUS Annual
Association for School, College and University Staffing
1600 Dodge Ave., S-330
Evanston, IL 60201

Job Seeker's Guide to Private and Public Companies (Detroit: Gale Group, 1995).

The Job Seeker's Guide to Socially Responsible Companies by Katherine Jankowski (Detroit: Gale Group, 1995).

Kennedy's Career Strategist
(monthly newsletter)
1150 Wilmette Ave.
Wilmette, IL 60091

Manufacturing Directories (Standish, ME: Tower International, annual).
Marketing and Sales Career Directory (Hawthorne, NJ: Career Press, 1992).
McFadden American Bank Directory (Skokie, IL: American Banker/Thomson Financial Publishing, 1994).
Medical and Health Information Directory (Detroit: Gale Group, 1999).
Merriam Webster's Medical Dictionary (Springfield, MA: Merriam Webster Inc. Publishing, 2002).
Million Dollar Directory: America's Leading Public and Private Companies (Bethlehem, PA: Dun & Bradstreet Information Services, 1993).
MTBI Step II Manual 2001 (Palo Alto, CA: Consulting Psychologists Press, 2001).

National Ad Search (weekly job ad newspaper)
National Ad Search, Inc.
Milwaukee, WI

National Association of Colleges and Employers (NACE) Salary Surveys (formerly *College Placement Council Annuals*) (Bethlehem, PA: NACE, annual).
National Directory of Internships (Raleigh, NC: National Society for Internships and Experiential Education, 1998).
National Directory of Non-Profit Organizations (Detroit: Gale Group, 2001).
National Directory of State Agencies (Bethesda, MD: Cambridge Information Group, 1989).
National Trade and Professional Associations of the United States by Buck Downs (Washington, DC: Columbia Books Inc., 2002).
Nelson's Directory of Investment Research by Marcia Boysen (Port Chester, NY: Nelson Information, 1999).
The New Complete Guide to Environmental Careers by Kevin Doyle (Washington, DC: Island Press, 1999).
NewsLinks (Princeton, NJ: International Schools Services, quarterly newsletter).
Non-Profit Job Finder by Daniel Lauber (River Forest, IL: Planning/Communications, 1994).

Occupational Outlook Handbook (Washington, DC: U.S. Department of Labor Bureau of Labor Statistics, 2002).

Occupational Outlook Quarterly (magazine) (Washington, DC: U.S. Department of Labor Bureau of Labor Statistics).

O'Dwyer's Directory of Public Relations Firms (New York: J.R. O'Dwyer Co. Inc., 2002).

The 100 Best Companies for Gay Men and Lesbians by Ed Mickens (New York: Pocket Books, 1994).

The 100 Best Companies to Sell For by Michael Harkavy and The Philip Lief Group (New York: John Wiley & Sons, 1989).

The 100 Best Companies to Work for in America by Robert Levering and Milton Moskowitz (New York: Bantam Doubleday Dell Publishing Group, Inc., 1994).

101 Challenging Government Jobs for College Graduates by William Shanahan (New York: Hungry Minds/Wiley, 1986)

Opportunities in Banking Careers (Chicago: VGM Career Books, 2000).

Opportunities in Government Careers (Chicago: VGM Career Books, 1992).

Opportunities in Health and Medical Careers (Chicago: VGM Career Books, 1998).

Opportunities in Human Resources Management Careers (Chicago: VGM Career Books, 1994).

Opportunities in Marketing Careers (Chicago: VGM Career Books, 1999).

Opportunities in Nonprofit Organizations Careers (Chicago: VGM Career Books, 1994).

Opportunities in Personnel Management Careers (Chicago: VGM Career Books, 1991).

Opportunities in Sales Careers (Chicago: VGM Career Books, 2001).

Opportunities in Technical Sales Careers (Chicago: VGM Career Books, 2001).

Opportunities in Telecommunications Careers (Chicago: VGM Career Books, 1995).

Opportunities in Television and Video Careers (Chicago: VGM Career Books, 1998).

Peterson's Graduate Schools in the U.S. (Princeton, NJ: Peterson's Guides, 2001).

Peterson's Grants for Graduate Students (Princeton, NJ: Peterson's Guides, 1998).

Peterson's Internships (Princeton, NJ: Peterson's Guides, 2003).

Places Rated Almanac by David Savageau (New York: General Reference and Travel, 2000).

Plunkett's Financial Services Almanac 2002–2003 (Houston: Plunkett Research Ltd.).

Plunkett's Retail Industry Almanac: The Only Complete Guide to the American Retail Industry and Its Major Firms by Jack W. Plunkett (Houston: Plunkett Research, Ltd., 2001–2002).

Professional Careers Sourcebook edited by Christine Maurer and Kathleen Savage (Detroit: Gale Group, 2000).

Professional's Job Finder by Daniel Lauber (River Forest, IL: Planning/Communications, 1997).

Public Relations Career Directory by Ronald W. Fry (Detroit: Gale Group, 1993).

Résumés for Sales and Marketing Careers (Chicago: VGM Career Books, 1999).

SIGI PLUS (interactive computer programming for career decision making)
Educational Testing Service
Princeton, NJ
sigi.ets.org

The Skills Search (video) (Indianapolis: JIST Publishing, 1992).

Sports Market Place (Princeton, NJ: Sportsguide, 1999).

Standard Directory of Advertising Agencies (New Providence, NJ: Reed Reference Publishing/National Register, 1999).

Standard and Poor's Register of Corporations (New York: Standard and Poor's Corp./McGraw-Hill, 2001).

State Government Research Directory by Kay Gill (Detroit: Gale Group, 1987).

Stedman's Medical Dictionary (Philadelphia: Lippincott, Williams and Wilkins, 2000).

Strong Interest Inventory Information
CPP, Inc.
Palo Alto, CA

Student Conservation Association
P.O. Box 550
Charlestown, NH 03603-0550

U.S. Industry and Trade Outlook (New York: McGraw-Hill Companies, 2000).

U.S. News and World Report (magazine) (Washington, DC).

Ward's Business Directory of Corporate Affiliations (Detroit: Gale Group, 2004).

Where the Jobs Are: A Comprehensive Directory of 1200 Journals Listing Career Opportunities by S. Norman Feingold and Glenda Hansard-Winkler (Garrett Park, MD: Garrett Park Press 1989).

Who Audits America, 47th ed. (Menlo Park, CA: Data Financial Press, 2000).

Who Will Care for Us? by Robyn Stone and Joshua Weiner (Washington, DC: American Association of Homes for the Aging, 2001).

World Chamber of Commerce Directory (Loveland, CO: World Chamber of Commerce Directory, 2002).

Y National Vacancy List
YMCA of the USA
Chicago, IL

Index

Directories
  for health care jobs, 52
  for nonprofit jobs, 171–72
Disney, 107, 108
Distribution, product, 93–94
Divisional merchandise managers (DMM), 120
Dogpile, 45
Dr. Martens, 108

E-commerce, 107
E-mail, 20, 29, 30, 47
E-retailing, 107
Earnings. *See* Salaries
Earth General, 109
Earth Mercantile, 109
Earth stores, 109
Economic needs, calculating your, 8–12
Eco-Wise, 109
Education section (of résumé), 23
Electronic Applicant Tracking, 31
Electronic résumés, 29–30
Employer(s)
  contacting, 45
  directories, 52
  personal traits preferred by, 24–25
  relating skills to, 15, 16
  repetitive employment with same, 25–26
  in retailing, 126–29
  several positions with same, 25–26
Entertainment, retailing and, 107–8
Entrepreneurship, 117
Environment, the
  nonprofit jobs related to, 161
  and retailing, 108–9
Environmental Careers Organization, 173
Executive director (of nonprofit organization), 158–59
Executive training programs, 115
Expenses, calculating your, 8–12
Experience section (of résumé), 24–27
Experiential diary, 14, 15, 57

FA (financial analyst), 186
Faxing, 20, 31
Feedback, 49
Finance consulting, 199
Financial analyst (FA), 186
501-c tax-exempt status, 156
Food Business Forum, 130
Food First Books, 171
Ford Motor Company, 41
Foreign languages, 145
Forward integration, 108
Frankel, Carl, 109
Functional résumé, 27

General merchandise managers (GMM), 120
General objective statement, 22
General skills, 14, 16
Geographically based directories, 52
GMM (general merchandise managers), 120
Goals
  for interviews, 59
  longer-term, 12–13
Grade point average (GPA), 23
"Green retailing," 109
Group work (in M.B.A. programs), 184

HandsNet, 173
Heading (of résumé), 20
Health care, 74–76, 133–53
  advancement in, 141
  business needs in, 75, 134–35
  and business sensitivity, 134–35, 138, 139
  career outlook for jobs in, 142–43
  as career path, 135–38
  changes in, 139
  communication skills in, 145
  costs of, 133–34
  degree requirements for, 136–37
  demographic factors in, 142
  earnings in, 141–42
  employment opportunities in, 143–45
  and finances, 143
  and foreign languages, 145
  home, 143
  jargon in, 137–38
  job sites, 138–39
  job sources for, 147–48
  job titles in, 148–49
  and marketing, 137
  networking in, 146
  positions in, 135–37
  professional associations related to, 150–53
  professional development in, 140–41
  reform of, 134
  related occupations, 149–50
  risk factors in, 139–40
  skills in, 75–76, 140, 145
  strategies for finding jobs in, 143–47
  and technology, 143
  training and qualifications for jobs in, 140
  working environment, 138–40
  working hours, 139
Health and Human Service departments, 144
Health maintenance organizations (HMOs), 135–36, 143
Herbergers, 127
Hidden job markets, 41–42
High school jobs, 26
Hiring practices, 62–63, 112
HMOs. *See* Health maintenance organizations
Hobbies, 6